# How to Pee Standing Up

## Tips for Hip Chicks

### BY ANNA SKINNER

### ILLUSTRATIONS BY SARA SCHWARTZ

doWn
tOwn
press

New York   London   Toronto   Sydney   Singapore

Written by Anna Skinner
Illustrated by Sara Schwartz
An *Original* Publication of POCKET BOOKS

A Downtown Press Book published by
POCKET BOOKS, a division of Simon & Schuster, Inc.
1230 Avenue of the Americas, New York, NY 10020

Produced by 17th Street Productions,
an Alloy company
151 West 26th Street
New York, NY 10001

ISBN: 0-7434-7024-9

First Downtown Press printing June 2003

10 9 8 7 6 5 4 3 2 1

DOWNTOWN PRESS and colophon are trademarks of Simon & Schuster, Inc.

Cover Design: Jennifer Blanc
Interior Design: Lauren Monchik

Printed in the U.S.A.

For information regarding special discounts for bulk purchases, please contact
Simon & Schuster Special Sales at 1-800-456-6798 or business@simonandschuster.com

**How to Pee Standing Up** isn't just about liberating yourself from skanky toilet seats. Nope. This little book aims higher than that. (Pardon the pun!) The survival tips you're about to read will teach you the kind of skills you need to be a "kick ass and take names" kind of female—tackling life's missions with attitude and finesse. So for those of you who want to be sneaky, not saintly; who kick butt, not kiss it (unless, of course, kissing it gets you one step up the ladder); who delight in being bad and doing good; and who always think of yourselves, please read on. And feel free to add a few tips of your own.

# TABLE OF CONTENTS

# BEAT THE BANK

**mission:**
**To pull yourself out of the red and into the black.**
**(And who doesn't look great in black?)**

So there you are, swinging through life buying a teensy bauble here, an itty-bitty new purse there, and occasionally taking that hottie down the hall to a nice little din-din to cheer him up after a lousy audition. "Everyone deserves a little pampering now and then," you tell yourself. Your friends tell you the same thing, sympathetically—especially when you're picking up the check. And that's when you get the call. You know the one—it's usually from a Mr. Green or a Ms. White, and it almost always begins with something misleadingly polite like, "We'd like to speak to you right away about your credit card balance." "Why are they bothering me?" you ask. "It was just a pair of shoes!" you think. And finally: "What's with the color-coded pseudonyms?"

We hate to inform you, but you've fallen into the dreaded Deadly Debt Trap. All credit cards should come with a label: Warning! Warning! Credit cards are not free money! But they don't, and before you know it, you're maxed out and have zero money left over after paying your bills. How's a person supposed to lead a fabulous life with a budget of nada?

## Stupid Reasons for Going into Credit Card Debt

1. Gucci brings out my green eyes.
2. With a big-screen TV like that, who needs a boyfriend?
3. My honey may be a deadbeat, but he's my little deadbeat!
4. Bloomingdale's is on my way to work. Like that's my fault.
5. By buying those Ralph Lauren sheets on sale, I'm actually saving money!

Having credit card debt is like wearing a heavy ankle bracelet (we're talking house arrest, not a fashion accessory) 24/7. It keeps you from building any kind of savings, including your See Ya Sucker Stash (see Hit the Road), and can make it harder for you to rent apartments, get loans, or buy a house.

## Proper Credit Card Conduct

1. Transfer your balances to cards that earn you freebies, like airline mileage.
2. Transfer your balances to a card that has an extremely low APR* (like no interest for a year), then try to pay it off before that introductory APR is raised.
3. Always pay more than the minimum, but not so much that you don't have enough to pay other bills.
4. Finally, screen your calls—no need to let "Mr. White" ruin your night. Just be sure to pay the bill the next day.

## Tips for Getting out of Debt

1. Don't live in denial. Figure out everything and everybody you owe.

2. Lower your expenses. Tap into your inner Disciplinarian, who can slap down your inner Princess from time to time. When you start to whip out the plastic, ask yourself: "Oh, fabulous one, is this a need or an indulgence?" Learn to tell the difference between the two; indulge when you have the cash in hand, but try to do it cheaply. (See Blue-Chip Babes.)

3. Increase your income. Get two jobs (it can be done) or a higher-paying gig until your debt is paid off.

4. Get help. Call the Consumer Credit Counseling Services at (800) 577-2227.

*APR: Aaah, a term we've all grown to know and love. It stands for **Annual Percentage Rate**—in other words, the cost of not paying off that balance. Hey, those credit card folks don't phone because they want to hear how your day went.

# Style on a Budget

offer to be a haircut model

from used Bookstores

Fajitas etc

90's style girl

Sea Salt

Olive

olive oil + rose oil

for Goddess Bath

cherry blood red nail Polish

RED red

creme fresh

Caspian Honey M

Spanish Olives

Some Extravagant delicacies

chill in fridge

champagne

# BLUE-CHIP BABE

A bad salary is worse than a rotten mission: A mission has a beginning and an end, but having a busted bank account can make you feel trapped. It can also send you into Debtor Hell, running up Visa accounts willy-nilly in an attempt to live large on a paycheck that isn't. Fact: Going into debt is never glamorous.

But it just isn't easy maintaining one's wicked ways on a budget that's more Bud and beans than cocktails and caviar. For those of you who know that true style is measured by how much your feet hurt, here are a few savvy tips.

## Style
Without glamour, we may as well be Jane Doe. And let's face it, Miss Jane is a dull girl.

11

You've cruised the Saturday night cineplex scene, but have you discovered the meditative charm of matinees? Sneak in your own chocolate treats and a cup of mint tea, instead of eating high-priced nachos and hot dogs of suspicious origin. You'll leave feeling restored—not rotund.

1. Offer to model for a hair salon (preferably one that doesn't have Super in its name), in exchange for free haircuts and highlights.

2. For cheap style ideas, cruise used bookstores for cool '50s and '60s cookbooks (for entertaining ideas) and '70s fashion and decor books (for funky style).

3. Carry your bad self into any high-end boutique or department store and try on the most expensive thing. If you lose your nerve, just pretend you're Courtney Love, the high priestess of brazenness. If you're really good, the sales staff will have no idea that you have exactly $19 in your checking account. This is also an excellent exercise in role playing.

4. Invest in two bottles of nail polish—I recommend Cherry Red for when you're feeling nice and Blood Red for naughtier times—nail polish remover, and a nail file. Give yourself weekly manicures and pedicures, changing colors to suit your mood. This will make you feel high-maintenance.

5. Buy a car that's vintage and stylish (like an old El Camino); this way, it will appear that your crappy car is really an aesthetic choice.

## Bathe Like a Goddess

Combine two cups of fine sea salt (at your grocery or health food store) with one ounce of oil (grapeseed, sweet almond, or olive) and six to eight drops of pure, essential oil (rose or lavender is nice). Mix well. Gently massage the salt all over your naked bod (excluding the face and neck), picking up what falls into the tub and reusing it. Then fill your tub with water.

# Shelter

Your shelter is the sanctuary in which you'll recover from the oh-so-draining pressure of a fabulous life on the go. These are small touches that can turn your modest little hovel into a full-on swankienda.

1. Always keep a bottle of champagne in your refrigerator, and be sure to toast yourself in the tub (hey, just for being you!) while you watch your toenails dry.

2. Keep a few extravagant food items in your refrigerator—like $12 brandied peaches from France or perishable Hawaiian honey. You don't have to open them; it's enough to know that they are there.

3. Subscribe to high-style "shelter" magazines instead of buying them on the stands (where 3 issues cost the same price as a year's subscription). You'll find excellent ideas about how the jet set decorate their villas, castles, and, well, jets.

4. Imbibe at home (preferably not alone) and only high-end liquors. You can make Sapphire (a color that looks great on everyone) martinis at home for less than $2 a tipple.

5. Find a male submissive in the personal columns, and order him to come clean your house.

Trade in your unwanted CDs (here's a tip: anything from your boy-band days) for new ones (such as the rockin' sounds of hipper boy-band The Strokes or the sexy grooves of Zero 7) at used record stores.

Some Extravagant delicacies

## Blue-Chip Babe Tip #2
Drop into a swank gym, and tell them you're interested in signing up but would like to try out the facilities first. Then have your very own day at the spa—and never go back. Hey, it's legal!

## Stepping Out

The social arena is a good place to test your disguises—with or without the troops.

1. Taxi! If you are carless, occasionally splurge on cab rides instead of schlepping it on the bus. You'll feel important, even if your destination is the dump where you flip burgers.

2. Here's a handy disguise with unlimited benefits (including discounts all over your town): the poverty-stricken student. Snag a student ID from a junior or city college by signing up for classes. Even if you drop out, you can keep the ID (and all of its perks).

3. Buy cheap-seat balcony tickets to the opera, ballet, symphony, or musicals (but only if it's *Cabaret*), and sneak down to the empty seats in the orchestra section during intermission. (For Advanced Operatives: Visit the Founders Room, where all the high rollers hang out, and act as if you belong there.*)

* Extra points if you score free drinks.

4. Take yourself to high tea at the swankiest restaurant or hotel in town once a month. It won't cost that much, and you'll feel like the glamorista you really are.

Another option: Get a job that gets you access. If you work for a magazine or a record company, you'll get invited to lots of parties and score freebies that will help offset the lousy pay.

5. Visit art openings at trendy galleries for free wine and elbow-rubbing with the arty types and wanna-bes. The art world has many subjects to study, especially if you're interested in the type who "longs to belong" but has no observable talent other than the gift of gab. (For Advanced Operatives: Scam your way into an after-opening dinner or party.)

## Personal Shopper, Please

If you're not into used closing stores and bargain bins, learn to consolidate your wardrobe purchases into two yearly outings. Save toward that preset date, and then use your budget to buy a few fashion essentials. Here's a little-known fact: Many clothing stores offer the services of a personal shopper—even the chains like Banana Republic. Call ahead and make an appointment. Once there, explain your needs—conservative job wear or funky fashion—and be firm about the amount you have to spend. Then your P.S. can recommend the three or four "must-haves" for the season and your wardrobe. It's a sensible way to stay up-to-date and keeps you from getting nickeled and dimed throughout the year on low-quality stuff you'll wear once and never use again.

## Skip the Meals Out

Perhaps the most important words in the vocabulary of a Blue-Chip Babe on a Budget are "No thanks. I ate earlier." Here's the deal: Drinks and fun = necessities of life. Twenty-five-dollar chicken plate = extravagance. There's no reason why you can't join everyone for the party after dinner. (Hey, that's when the fun really begins anyway.) So learn to feed yourself at home, then join your friends later.

### Blue-Chip Babe Tip #3
Find a fancy hotel and sneak a swim in its heated pool. Note: This is equally satisfying if done alone or with another Operative. Ultrasatisfying if done with a very buff operative.

15

# BOSS FROM HELL

**mission:**
To survive the workplace when the head honcho is a creep.
Extra points for getting him or her fired.

Let's face it—a rotten boss can be one of life's biggest drags. Having such a boss means you will be faced with someone you find repellent on a daily basis, often before you've had any coffee. Worse, you will be forced to be civil to this person, even smile at this person, and generally avoid throwing anything heavy in his or her direction. For an employee who's used to expressing her opinion, occasionally by throwing things, this situation can quickly become torturous.

After considerable experience with the dreaded Boss from Hell, we have found that they fall into one of four categories—the Moron, the Power Perv, the Passive-Aggressive, and the Bully—with frequent crossovers occurring. *Note: If you find yourself facing a boss who is a combination of all the aforementioned categories, you should regard the situation as hopeless. Find yourself a good headhunter, and get the hell out of there.*

**The following characteristics indicate the presence of an official Boss from Hell.**

You know you're dealing with a Boss from Hell when he or she:

* Reams you for coming in five minutes late, then calls you "Baby Cakes" five minutes later.
* Asks you to brainstorm some ideas, but stares silently at you when you do.
* Steals your ideas without giving you credit.
* Takes too much of a creepy interest in your personal life.
* Hires you, then doesn't speak to you again for the next three months.
* Only notices your mistakes, and likes to mention them loudly in the break room.
* Throws tantrums with no provocation.
* Throws tantrums with provocation.
* Sets you up to take the fall.
* Doesn't describe what is expected of you and then yells when you don't "do your job."
* Asks you to cover while he or she plays hooky.
* "Forgets" to pay you overtime.
* Guilt-trips you for taking maternity leave.
* Chases you around the desk—or anything else—in the office.
* Asks you to do a cocaine run.

## The Moron

By moron, we mean the kind of boss who says astonishingly stupid things with equally astonishing frequency. This is the mildest type of Bad Boss, but that doesn't mean he or she won't drive you bananas. Instead of stressing about it, write down the stupidest comments, and tell yourself you'll write a book one day. Also, take comfort in the fact that you will clearly take this boss's job in a matter of months, if not days.

## THE POWER PERV

How bad can these bosses be? The following tragic story is true. The names have not been changed, in the hopes that the employee whose story it is may reap maximum vengeance.

"My mission began when Burt, a wealthy German financial planner, decided to get in the movie biz and hired me as his production assistant. My duties, in addition to typing his memos, were to prepare his morning drink of green tea made from twigs. Since I didn't like fetching drinks for people who signed my paychecks, I'd space out and sometimes boil his tea for too long. He would get worked up and accuse me of trying to kill him; it wasn't long before I started doing it on purpose *[an oldie-but-goodie passive-aggressive Double-Agent trick]*. Burt's favorite thing to do, besides bitch about his tea, was to talk about sex. He was married to a hippie chick thirty years his junior, and he claimed they had an 'open marriage.' *[Note: This term, coming from a boss, should be taken as a red flag.]*

"Burt began to insist that I eat lunch with him at his favorite Thai place. He'd sit and talk about his experiences in Thai brothels, boasting that he always had two girls *[puh-leaze!]*. It wasn't long after that when he began to stare at my breasts and slowly invade my personal space while talking to me. I would have quit, but I needed the money and didn't have another job lined up. One day, old Burt finally snapped and began chasing me around the office—*[a clichéd but not uncommon sitch]*. Finally, when I was trapped between him and my desk, I raised my hand, warning him to stop. The next thing I knew, the creep grabbed my pinky finger and bent it back. This was clearly a weird seduction move—even for lechy Burt—to say nothing of the fact that it hurt like hell. That was it for me: I slugged him in the bicep. *[See Self-Defense.]* Burt grabbed his arm and slithered back to his office. After that, he laid off for about a month. And by the time he started leering at me again, I had already given notice."

—as told by a happily self-employed Operative

## Five Ways to Stop the Power Perv

1. Tell the P.P. to cut it out. Simple but surprisingly effective, this move is important because Pervs are capable of reading a come-on into every comment, no matter how benign. (You say, "Can you hand me my coffee cup?" He hears, "Would you find a way to brush your hand against my chest?") So be direct: "This is making me uncomfortable, and I want to keep the door open." That's hard to misinterpret, even for a Power Perv.

2. Document, document, document. If Step #1 doesn't work, you'll need backup for the eventual complaint.

3. File a complaint with your Human Resources department. If he still can't keep his hands to himself, go to a supervisor and give him up.

4. Punch the Power Perv. *Note: Only recommended for hand-to-hand combat situations similar to previous page. Otherwise, you'll just have to fantasize about it.*

5. File a harassment suit. With your settlement, fly to Costa Rica and write that tell-all novel, exacting maximum revenge.


**THE PASSIVE-AGGRESSIVE**

Passive-Aggressive bosses don't tell you what you need to know to do your job successfully. Ever fearful of confrontation, the P.A. will never criticize you to your face, but she or he *will* talk trash behind your back.

Remember the 3 F's when dealing with classic Passive-Aggressive foes:

## 1. Flattery

When in doubt, flatter (one of our favorites). If the P.A. is female, she'll feel like you recognize her innate fabulousness. If the P.A. is male, well, ditto.

> Sample Comment: "My favorite part of the presentation was that hilarious accounting anecdote you told at the end. How did you ever come up with it?"

## 2. Forge Ahead

If he or she is procrastinating in giving you the info you need to complete a project, see the job through to completion on your own and deal with the fallout later. *Note: Feel free to play the Flattery card here, too.*

*Extra points for combination of **Forging** and **Flattery.***

> Sample Comment: "I went ahead and called Steve for those numbers. I laid them out the same way you did in your last report—I thought it was much more clear." *

## 3. Facts

Always keep your boss posted in writing (memos, e-mail) of everything you're working on. And when she pisses you off, which she undoubtedly will, don't fly off the handle. Instead, calmly discuss the facts.

> Sample Comment: "I'm sorry you're surprised that I turned the report in before you had a chance to see it. If you'll check your e-mails and the note I left on your desk, you'll see I did let you know that I was working on it and that I would turn it in on Monday."

## THE BULLY

This type of boss is the most easily identified of the four types—usually by how often he or she throws desk objects or coffee mugs across the room.

Mr. Boss

Bully Bosses come in many shapes and sizes—screamers and threateners, male and female. Similarly, the Bully is not discriminating when it comes to choosing a victim. But you can bet that if you are popular, competent, or given to high moral standards and solid integrity, you will be a prime target. The Bully Boss will see you as a potential threat and attack with a vengeance (and in the worst cases, with a stapler). What triggers an outburst? Sticking up for someone who's being victimized in the office, challenging the status quo, or—most dangerously—showing the potential to expose your boss's lousy job performance.

Since Bully Bosses are usually completely incapable of normal social interaction, they rely on their formidable skills of deception. B.B.'s generally don't have real talent; they've found other ways to make it to Boss-dom. That's why they are usually adept at lying and at escaping accountability for their actions. Combine these characteristics with their habits of dispensing relentless criticism, undermining comments, ridiculous workloads, and unrealistic deadlines, and it's enough to break even the toughest employee.

## Steps You Can Take to Counter the Bully Boss

1. Write down every instance of bullying and keep it private. (Operative Lesson 101: Do not leave this valuable information on the hard drive of your computer at work.)

2. Save any bullying correspondence (e-mails, memos, etc.). When the Bully makes yet another idiotic accusation, ask for evidence supporting his stupid claim and even ask him to put it in writing. He'll probably back down like the coward he is, but if he keeps it up, let him know—again, in writing—that making unsubstantiated allegations is a form of harassment.

3. If he forces it, go the Tattletale route. Talk to personnel and file a complaint. Try to stay away from personal or

opinionated complaints. ("She's a cretin and has a cheap haircut" won't get you anywhere.) Instead, coolly concentrate on the Bully Boss's actions, and show them the evidence. Note: Human Resources usually sides with upper management as long as the department is performing well. Also, don't forget: Bullies are exceptional liars.

4. If Step #3 fails, call in the Mouthpiece. Talk to a lawyer.

5. Of course, if you've gotten to Step #4, you'll probably be on your way out. At some point, a wise girl knows when to move on.

*Boss from Hell Fact:*
Bully Bosses rarely change. When you quit, they will find a new target.

# BREAKUP

### mission:

**To survive a breakup with your mind, body, and spirit intact—
and without losing any of your good CDs.**

Breakups can be dangerous terrain. A bad breakup (usually the kind where you're the Breakup-ee) can make you feel puny (and occasionally vengeful—see Revenge); a good one (usually the kind where you're the Breakup-er) can be one big sigh of relief.

A really bad breakup story:

Once upon a time, there was a girl in love (let's call her Jane Schmo), whose boyfriend suggested they get his-and-hers tattoos. At the tattoo parlor, her boyfriend (we'll call him Dick Little) insisted she go first. So Jane gritted her teeth while Dick's name was etched onto her backside. When the tattoo was finished, Dick checked it out to make sure his name was spelled right (how many ways can you spell Dick?), then announced that he was dumping Jane and walked out of the tattoo parlor and Jane's life for good.

\*    \*    \*

The moral of this story? Don't date a Dick!

Sorry—another way to look at it is that if a guy dumps you, he's not worth your time and certainly not worthy of you, so just be thankful you didn't tattoo his name on your ass.

Here's a question: Is it worse to be the Dumper or the Dumpee? Sure it hurts to get the heave-ho, but sometimes it's even crappier to be the one doing the heaving. Your ego isn't as banged up, but you're left with all the responsibility (and guilt). Here are some basic strategies to manage your way through both ends of a Big Breakup.

(ditch memories)

## DUMPER DON'TS:

1. Don't take on the dreaded guilt trip! **Staying with someone out of pity is gross, not to mention downright selfish. Think of it this way: You're cheating your would-be ex—and yourself—out of moving on to the Next Great Thing. You may think you're doing someone a favor by sticking around beyond the Bitter End, but let's face it: That last queasy month or two will only bring sour feelings and a couple of episodes of really bad sex. Wake-up call: Change is the only constant in life. Move on.**

> **Dating After a Breakup**
> Spit out that bitter pill. Keep your heart open when you start to date again. Don't hold the sins of the ex against a potential new hottie.

2. **Don't draw it out by having looong talks with the Dumpee about what went wrong, whose fault it was, why you've changed, blah, blah, blah. It makes us tired just writing about those conversations. (Can you picture Foxy Brown doing that relationship rap? We**

## Breakup Tip #1

Sometimes it's easier to take the blame for breaking up a relationship than it is to try to explain why your boyfriend's ear hair really bugs you. On the other hand, this method is not appropriate if the significant other has done something really heinous. In that case, you are free to tell him exactly why you'd rather be sentenced to wear culottes and clogs for the rest of your life than spend another minute as his main squeeze.

didn't think so.) Here's the deal: Be nice (remind your Dumpee of what makes him or her so great), but be firm about your intentions (and the clear steps you're ready to take—i.e., giving him a deadline for moving out). And never let the talk degenerate into a blame game.

3. Don't try to stay friends. This is a classic trap we've all fallen into, so read this closely: Instead of making your ex feel "safe" by sticking around, you are making him or her feel like crap. Cut the ties that bind.

4. Don't recycle. Too many of us end up repeating the same relationship missteps over and over again. In other words, think long and hard about what it was that turned you off about your ex. The reasons could be deep (he's selfish) or, let's face it, shallow (he wears acid-washed jeans). Either way, learn to avoid Mr. Selfish Acid-Wash Guy (or whatever your peculiar little weakness is) in the next go-round.

## DUMPEE DO'S:

1. Do break off all contact. The Setup: You tell yourself that you just want to talk to him, that it's easier if you "stay friends." The Fall: There you are, having a beer somewhere as "friends," when suddenly you bust out crying right into your pale ale and embarrass you both by asking to have his baby. Instead of humiliating yourself, box all those pictures of you and "Honey" (and anything else that's a reminder) and throw them

in the back of your closet until you get hold of your tender self.

2. Do wallow in self-pity. Hey— it's good for you! By letting yourself feel miserable, you're helping the healing process along. So download a Patsy Cline box set, and get real down-and-dirty pitiful, if only for the night.

**Breakup Tip #2**
**Never drink and dial.** Here's a guarantee: The moment your ex picks up the phone, you'll feel like a total loser— especially when he or she hangs up on you.

3. Do pamper yourself silly. Here's a to-do list of doctor-recommended therapies for the recently dumped:
   * Get a massage.
   * Buy self flowers.
   * Purchase wildly sexy top/shoes/lingerie and revel in your sensuality. (You're still sexy even though you're partner-free!)
   * Listen to righteous-type music.
   * Convene best friends for revenge-fantasy session.
   * Treat self to vacation, or if broke, treat self to movie filmed in preferred vacation setting.
   * Hug pet; swear to pet it will be most important partner from now on.
   * Eat recklessly unhealthy foods.
   * Keep nails painted in I-Will-Survive-and-Conquer red.
   * Revel in shamelessly luxurious hot baths.

4. Do reconnect with yourself. Shift your perspective from "I just got dumped" to "What the hell did I learn from this (besides 'never date a man prettier than me')?" Take long hikes, see a therapist, try something new (knitting, painting, acting, karate).

5. Do rebound, rebound, rebound. There's nothing like a little fling to boost that ego after a dumping. Sometimes the gods drop little surprises into your lap right when you need them most. Just make sure it's a no-harm rebound, meaning not with your ex's brother, father, or best friend.

## Big, Bad Breakup No-No's

You know you're handling your breakup poorly if any of the following happens:
- Your ex calls the cops and/or obtains a restraining order.
- You set anything on fire.
- You tap into your ex's voice mail or e-mail (although this move is slightly admirable for demonstrating surveillance skills).
You know who you are. Calm down and get some help.

### The Yo-Yo:

This form of ex is the most destructive of all. He convinces you that he can't exist without you (it's the poetry that always sucks you in, am I right?), then forgets your next two dates. Avoid this one like the plague—he'll wipe out your self-esteem faster than you can say, "I'll have a gallon of Cherry Garcia in a cup, please."

# DIAL-UP

### mission:
**To bilk the phone company out of your
long-distance nickel. Better yet, it's legal!**

There's nothing a savvy girl loves more than getting something
for nothing. Especially if that something involves chatting with friends in
exotic places like Monaco, Mozambique, and Toledo. And if you're already
paying for an Internet connection, you'll be happy to know that you never
have to pay for another long-distance call again. Listen up:  Getting free
long distance is almost as good as getting free shoes. Almost.

## The Deal:
They call it Internet telephony (but you can call it Internet long distance),
and it works something like this: If you have a computer and an Internet connection (like Earthlink or AOL), you can go to an Internet LD site (see The
Sites to See in this chapter), download their software, and talk to your
compadre in Kansas for free, even if you live in Hawaii. (We wish we were
in Hawaii. We love Hawaii.) Connections can be made from PC to PC

(provided your callee has the right software) or PC to phone, depending on the vendor you use. *Note: Telephony setups are geared mainly to PCs right now, but there are a few vendors that offer programs for Macs.*

## The Catch:

There always is one, isn't there? Internet long distance still has some kinks. Potential problems: poor sound quality and/or a bad connection. So while telephony may be ideal for chats with friends and good old Aunt Myrna (where sometimes a poor connection can be a good thing), we don't recommend it for business calls. Shop around: If one program doesn't work for you, try another.

*Dial-Up Tip #1*

For the clearest sound, get a high-quality headset with a built-in microphone. *Note: High-quality doesn't necessarily mean the most expensive. Shop around and compare.*

*Dial-Up Tip #2*

The faster your modem speed, the better. Make sure yours is at least 56 kbps. If you have a cable or DSL connection, you're in great shape.

*Dial-Up Tip #3*

Make sure your sound card is full-duplex. You can use the microphone and speakers that come with it, but you're better off with the headset, which can block out external noise.

## The Sites to See

Internet long-distance vendors are like many other Web sites; often here today and gone tomorrow. Listed below are available vendors as of this printing.

- iConnectHere *(http://www.iconnecthere.com)*
- Dialpad *(http://www.dialpad.com)*
- HotTelephone.com *(http://www.hottelephone.com)*
- MediaRing *(http://www.mediaring.com/index.phtml)*
- Net2Phone *(http://www.net2phone.com)*
- PhoneFree.com *(http://www.phonefree.com)*
- BuddyPhone *(http://www.buddyphone.com)*
- CallServe—for Europe *(http://www.callserve.com/langselect.asp)*

Not all of these sites offer free programs. But if you have to pay, it'll be a small amount (a penny a minute, as opposed to 5 to 7 cents a minute, which is what most telephone companies charge).

# DITCH THE DATE

## mission:
**To identify a lame date before it even starts;
to escape one with maximum flair.**

## First Step: Identification
### TYPES OF BAD DATES

After careful (and frequently painful) studies, we've found that most bad dates fall into one of a few distinct categories.

CLASSIFICATION: **The Loser Boozer**

IDENTIFYING REMARK: "Sorry, dude. I'm too frunk to duck."

IDENTIFYING BEHAVIOR: Parties seven nights a week; talks about partying seven nights a week; is a dud in the sack; has really bad breath from drinking, smoking, and booger sugar.

CLASSIFICATION: **The Grandson of Sam (aka "The Serial Killer")**

IDENTIFYING REMARK: "How do you feel about pain?"

LuV the hair?

IDENTIFYING BEHAVIOR: Guards his plate with a knife and fork; tells stories about torturing animals when he was little; has a temper that's easily triggered by weird things, like too much salt in his food or the color blue; insists that Manson got a bad rap; looks like the guy next door; knows too much about your shower routine.

CLASSIFICATION: **The Eye Candy**

IDENTIFYING REMARK: "Do you like my hair?"

IDENTIFYING BEHAVIOR: Stares blankly; giggles constantly; finds ingenious ways to check himself out in his silverware.

CLASSIFICATION: **The Two-Timing Tomcat**

IDENTIFYING REMARK: "What ring?"

IDENTIFYING BEHAVIOR: Can only see you on certain days; has a white strip on his wedding finger; seems in a hurry for sex; has monogrammed luggage.

CLASSIFICATION: **The Cell-Phone Addict**

IDENTIFYING REMARK: "Hold, please."

IDENTIFYING BEHAVIOR: Takes a call while you're on the date; makes a call when you're on the date; calls someone when you're stomping out the door; never calls again.

CLASSIFICATION: **The U.F.O. (Unidentified Foolish Operative)**

IDENTIFYING REMARK: "Have you ever been to Roswell?"

IDENTIFYING BEHAVIOR: Refers to himself as a 'droid; tries to flatter you by saying someone must have shot you with a phaser set on "hottie"; says he'd like to beam you up to his starship.

CLASSIFICATION: **The Bulldozer**

IDENTIFYING REMARK: "You know you like it."

IDENTIFYING BEHAVIOR: Orders "a nice rack" for dinner; introduces

Hooters

you as "my old lady"; asks your breasts what they do for a living.

CLASSIFICATION: **The Wet Noodle**
IDENTIFYING REMARK: "Sorry, I guess I'm a little tired."
IDENTIFYING BEHAVIOR: Lets you kiss him but pulls your hand away if you try to do more; waits for you to make all the first moves.

CLASSIFICATION: **The Home Boy**
IDENTIFYING REMARK: "I'd invite you in, but my parents are sleeping."
IDENTIFYING BEHAVIOR: Loves comic books; can't take you out because he has to do chores for his parents; probably plays in a band.

CLASSIFICATION: **The Cheap Bastard**
IDENTIFYING REMARK: "Does five sound OK? Happy hour ends at seven."
IDENTIFYING BEHAVIOR: Rushes ahead of you at the movies and buys his own ticket; says he has only $10 on him since he didn't have time to get his check cashed.

CLASSIFICATION: **The Adolescent**
IDENTIFYING REMARK: "What's your favorite video game?"
IDENTIFYING BEHAVIOR: Stays late at work to play PlayStation with other juvenile coworkers; takes pride in the length of his burps; tends to change fashion statements at the drop of a hat (from baggy pants and Caesar 'do to rock 'n' roll-tattooed-waif thing).

CLASSIFICATION: **The New Ager**
IDENTIFYING REMARK: "Your aura looks lovely tonight."
IDENTIFYING BEHAVIOR: Burns sage in your apartment before he goes out with you; tells you his spirit guide said that you would be "very special"; says your cat keeps smiling at him; introduces you as his "mystic lady"; has B.O.

> *Bad Date Tip #1*
> When the date gets tough, the gal gets going. To avoid getting stranded, always bring money for cab fare and the phone number of a cab company.

CLASSIFICATION: **The Player**

IDENTIFYING REMARK: "Your mom is hot!"

IDENTIFYING BEHAVIOR: Offers the "best massage you've ever had in your life" before he even tells you his last name; used to date your sister; used to date your cousin; says he knows the best free clinic in town.

CLASSIFICATION: **The Stoner**

IDENTIFYING REMARK: "Boobs, doobs, and tube."

IDENTIFYING BEHAVIOR: Gets into discussions about who's better—the Stones or Zep; generally apathetic; likes to stimulate the brain without moving the body (listening to music, watching TV); explores the Web's innermost quadrants in an effort to find the most arcane sites; loves trivia.

# Second Step: The Escape
## BAD-DATE BREAKOUTS

Of course, once a truly bad date has been identified, a real woman knows how to get the hell out. Once you've established that you are indeed on a first-class lame date (rule of thumb: would you rather be doing your taxes?), you'll need to know the exit strategy that works for you.

### 1. THE WRAP-IT-UP

For dates that have zero chemistry but aren't entirely hellish.

This kind of date should be looked at as being in prison for just a short sentence. You suffer for a designated period of time (15, 30, or 60 minutes—long enough to be civil, short enough to keep from getting hostile), then cut out with an excuse and an apology.

### Bad Date Tip #2

When stuck on a bad date, some of us find it useful to chat up hotties when our date's back is turned (being the resourceful types that we are). It's a little ego boost, not to mention a way to meet someone you really like. We fully recommend this, but only if you can do it on the sly.

"I have a huge presentation due tomorrow and need to work on it."

"I completely forgot that I have to drop some important papers off at my folks' house, and they go to bed at nine. Sorry."

## 2. THE RUNAWAY

*For more serious situations, like psychos and body builders.*

Excuse yourself and head for the ladies' room. Call a friend, tell her to wait 15 minutes, then call the restaurant (or wherever you are) and have you paged. If you can't reach your friend, nab your server and clue them in—they'll gladly participate in your scheme if only to alleviate the tedium of waiting tables (see Greasing the Palm). If you brought your own car, apologize, pay for whatever you've ordered, and make a run for it. If you came with your date, ask your friend (or your new friend the server) to call a cab for you so it's waiting outside. (Your date will think it was coincidence.) If a cab's not an option (see Bad Date Tip #1), you'll have to ask your date to take you home pronto.

*The Excuse*

"I feel really nauseous [probably not a complete lie] and have to leave now!" Tip: Clutch your stomach for extra emphasis. Also, if you tell him you feel like you're gonna throw up, there's no way your date will want to come in.

## 3. THE FREAKOUT

*For dates that are so unbearably dull, you need to shock just for the thrill of it.*

If you find yourself so bored that you can't even remember your date's name, it's time to employ this surefire date-repellent. Bring up a topic that will guarantee a quick wrap-up to the evening. Tip: The more creative you are with these conversational bombs, the more fun you'll have. For instance, "It's so nice to be on a date since my boyfriend got locked up—good thing he gets out tomorrow," or "Geez, my herpes is really bothering me tonight."

# EVIL LANDLORD

mission:
**To keep your tenant-landlord relationship
free of ill will, serious conflict, or letter-bombs.**

When the roaches in your apartment become more like roommates than occasional visitors (bad sign: when you begin to name them), who are you gonna call? The landlord, and usually he or she will take care of the problem. But this section isn't about those landlords. It's about the other kind—the ones who make you want to fake your own death just to get out of your lease. So learn how to protect yourself from this insidious adversary.

Your landlord is required to keep your unit in habitable condition. Here's what that means:

1. A sound building structure, including floors, roofs, and stairways.
2. Safe electrical, heating, and plumbing systems.
3. A reasonable supply of hot and cold water.
4. Terminating a pest infestation. Of course, if the problem is a

result of your sloppy living habits (like leaving trails of Krispy Kreme doughnut crumbs from the kitchen to the TV), you will foot the bill.

For problems like mildewed grout, broken blinds, or peeling paint—in other words, stuff that won't kill you but is a major decor drag—your landlord may or may not have an obligation to fix them. Always check:

1. your lease to see if the terms agree to maintaining these types of repairs.
2. state and local building codes.
3. landlord-tenant laws.
4. any promises your landlord has made, either verbal or written.

Minor repair problems? Here's the beef. *Note: These tactics are for evil landlords only. If your landlord is the type who will fix things without being harassed, threatened, or begged, thank your lucky stars. You must have done something nice in a past life.*

And now for the serious stuff . . .

**Fact:** Landlords will NOT change the color of your carpet from industrial gray to ivory shag. **Cosmetic changes are not their deal.**

## 1. WRITE A LETTER

Clearly state the nature of the problem, focusing on why it's in your landlord's best interest to take care of it. Speak in a language he understands—Cash Money. In other words, if he doesn't take care of the hole in the carpet, someone could trip and hurt herself, leaving him open to a fat lawsuit. Or the peeling paint in the bathroom could eventually turn into a mildewed wall, which means replacing the whole

## Evil Landlord Tip #1

In some states, tenants are allowed to deduct the amount of a repair from their rent. But check the laws carefully before resorting to this tactic. It's strictly a last-ditch attempt to force the Evil One into action. Once you've established you're within your rights to withhold the rent, write the landlord to inform him that this is your plan. Then head to the local courthouse and file the necessary papers for withholding the rent. Deposit the rent in an escrow account maintained by the court or a mediating service. Tip: Keeping the rent there—rather than going to Barney's and depositing it in the "new shoes account"—will look better to a judge.

damn thing down the road. If the problem affects other tenants, make the landlord aware of it. The advantage of writing a letter is that the landlord is less likely to automatically say, "Forget it!" Plus, you've got a paper trail.

## 2. HAVE A LITTLE TALK

If your letters and telephone calls are ignored, contact a mediation service. You can find them in the yellow pages under, um, "Mediation Services." This is a less expensive alternative to going to court, since many community mediators are free—or almost free. This process works pretty much the same way it did when you were a kid and your mom "mediated" your more hysterical sibling conflicts. (Except without the screeching. At least not as much.) The three of you will sit down, you'll tell your side of the story (just the facts, please), and your landlord will tell his. In a perfect world, the mediator will then tell the landlord what a cretin he is, and you'll be completely vindicated. Since this is a far-from-perfect world, chances are he'll come up with a fair compromise.

## 3. SEE YOU IN SMALL CLAIMS

Obviously, this is a worst-case solution. The reality is, once the relationship between you and your evil landlord has moved into court, you probably won't want to live in your place anymore. But if you really want to stay in your apartment—if it's rent-controlled, for example—you may have to fight it out. The lowdown: If you can prove that your unit's value has decreased due to the lack of repairs, a judge may find in your favor. This doesn't mean you'll be sailing to the Riviera on a big, fat judgment. Rather, the award will be determined by subtracting the monthly amount your unit is actually worth from what you've been paying for rent since you've had the problem. You get the difference.

## Search Me?

Landlords have the right to enter your apartment in the following situations:
• if there's an emergency,
• to make repairs, or
• to show the apartment to prospective tenants.
Most states require a 24-hour notification if the landlord wants to enter the apartment. Landlords may not enter your apartment to water your plants, check to see if you have enough to eat, or make your bed.

## How to Break Your Lease

Obviously, a lease is a written contract specifying, among other things, that you will stay in your apartment for a specific period of time. So how do you get out of it?

* If your landlord significantly violates the lease, you can break it.
* Some states have laws that allow a tenant to break a lease for health

reasons or job relocation. So if you want to break the lease in order to get a bigger and better apartment in another part of town, lie! Tip: Crying while lying sometimes helps your case.

*Note: Often it's easy for the landlord to re-rent the apartment right away—especially if you help line up a new tenant. So breaking your lease may turn out to be a breeze.*

# FIRST CLASS

**mission:**
To find airfare that's cheap enough to have money
left over for cocktails on the plane.

Nothing gets us high like soaring 35,000 feet above ground
on cut-rate airfare. Getting a bargain-basement fare is a tricky business,
and navigating the world of discount fares takes some primo hustling skills.

## When can you get discounted fares? When you travel:

1. For a funeral or for a family emergency. Like to see a close relative
   who's suddenly fallen ill. Airlines call them "sympathy" fares and
   will drop rates as low as 50% to 70% ; ask to speak with a
   manager if the reservations agent says they don't offer them.
2. For a wedding. Airlines will give bulk discount rates for out-
   of-town guests.
3. As a student. Be prepared to show an ID (see First Class).
4. With a senior citizen. You can get a discount, but this only
   works for one accompanying passenger.

# The Courier Caper

If you have a flexible schedule, don't mind traveling light, and are into exploring new destinations on your own, consider being a courier. Airfares are rock-bottom cheap (sometimes free), and you can travel to exotic locales like Europe, Australia, South America, Asia, and Africa.

## THE DEAL:

When you act as a courier, you accompany air freight and make sure it gets delivered to an air courier representative once you reach the destination. You can book flights in advance, or save even more $$$ by being able to leave at the last moment. You need to live near a major city (Los Angeles, Chicago, New York, San Francisco, or Miami), be 18, and have a passport.

## THE HOW-TO:

To become a courier, you have to pay an annual membership fee (usually under $50) to a company that has access to courier flight information.

## DID YOU KNOW?

If you checked in on time and are involuntarily bumped from your flight, you are eligible for compensation. If the airline puts you on another flight (same airline or different one) that gets you to your destination between one and two hours later than your originally scheduled flight, you're entitled to compensation (usually flight vouchers) equal to the price of your one-way fare, up to a maximum of $200. More than two hours late? That maximum doubles to $400.

*First Class Tip #2*
To get cheaper rates, start your travel on a Tuesday, Wednesday, or Thursday and stay overnight on a Saturday.

## Scams We Love—and Airlines Hate!

### SCAM #1: THE FLY-THROUGH

If you're trying to get from point A to point B, you may not want to buy a ticket from point A to point B. Do some research: You might save money if you buy a ticket that goes from point A to C, with a "pit stop" at point B. It's a sneaky little move called a "fly-through" that the savviest flyers know and love. *Note: It does violate the regulations of some airlines, so be sure to check the fine print.*

**Courier Organizations**
Air Courier Association
(www.aircourier.org)
Jupiter Air (www.jupiterair.com)
International Association of Air Travel Couriers
(www.courier.org)

### SCAM #2: MERCI BEAUCOUP!

If you're flying to Europe for a wildly glamorous adventure, instead of flying from, say, Los Angeles to London round-trip, book a departing flight from L.A. to London and (here's the sneaky part) a returning flight from Paris to Los Angeles. In other words, fly into one city and out of another. (It's called flying "open jaws.") You may save some moolah (especially if the U.S. dollar is stronger than the currency in the country where you bought your ticket), and avoid unnecessary extra traveling costs. *Trés* smart.

*First Class Tip #3*
Always carry your valuables—like jewelry, electronics (computers), or cash—on you when you fly. If your baggage is lost, you won't be reimbursed for these items. Frankly, we think carry-on is always the way to go, since life is too short to wait around staring at a conveyor belt, and bags invariably get lost during transfer flights.

# FRIENDSHIP FIXES

## mission:
**To manage your friendships with kindness,
tolerance, and the occasional whack upside the head.**

Friends can bring fun, excitement, and impromptu road trips to one's life. (We love impromptu road trips.) That's the good stuff. We also know they can bring annoying habits, stupid spats, and pesky complications, too. Yes, as with all good things, there's a price to pay for the company of a quality sidekick. Here's how to manage a few of the most classic friendship flare-ups.

### HOW TO: Go Separate Ways

SCENARIO: You grew up with Tonya. But as you've grown older, she's begun to morph into the kind of chick who wears headbands and quotes Oprah, while you just got your third body part pierced. Clearly, you and Tonya have grown apart. It's time to let you both off the hook.

## Dumping a Friend in 3 Easy Steps

1. Talk to Tonya one-on-one. Never give the heave-ho by telephone or (worse) by leaving a message or (the worst!) by sending an e-mail.
2. Tell Tonya you feel like the relationship isn't working. Give her specific examples (without being nasty—no need to be insulting), as well as a chance to respond.
3. If you still want out once you've talked awhile, tell her you think it's best if you take a break from each other for a little while.

### Friendship Fix Tip #1

Not all friends will be Ethel to your Lucy. Sometimes we do grow apart and want to do a little spring cleaning. Don't torture yourself about it—hey, chances are she's tired of you, too.

HOW TO: **Get Her Back**

SCENARIO: Crap. You've just made a spectacular, vodka-inspired mistake that involved your buddy's studly ex, four Jell-O shots, and a long night that ended with you and Mr. Stud Guy watching the sun come up from a chaotic backseat. (When you make a mistake, you do it big.) Now, in the bitter light of day and an epic hangover, you realize it's time to seriously sweet-talk your friend. Here's how:

## Winning a Friend Back in 5 Easy Steps

1. Call your friend and tell her you've made a hideous, mind-boggling boo-boo. (No, not the one about losing your shoes the night before. That was a different mistake.) Tell her exactly what you did (blurt it out fast, before you lose your nerve). Follow up by saying that you're sorry. Sorrier than you've ever been, in fact.
2. What you say next depends on how she reacts. If she hasn't hung up on you, tell her you realize that you've hurt her

and you hate that more than anything. Then ask to get together to talk.

3. Be sincere. Master the art of being apologetic without groveling. (If that doesn't work, go ahead and grovel.)
4. Don't expect her to forgive you right away. Recognize that her feelings may not have healed yet—give her time.
5. Sending flowers never hurts.

HOW TO: **Tell a Friend Something She Doesn't Want to Hear**

SCENARIO: You and Juanita watch each other's backs. But lately you feel like she's turned into a real downer. She complains nonstop and backstabs your other friends. Frankly, the girl's bad mood is driving you crazy.

## Tell a Friend She's Bugging You in 3 Easy Steps

1. Use the old "Sugar First" strategy. Before you slam your friend, tell her what you do like about her. Tell her that you love hanging out with her but that you have to talk with her about something that's bugging you.
2. Tell her what's on your mind, and be specific: "Janelle, did you really have to throw up on my mom at graduation?"
3. Prepare yourself—this is the part where she may go off, usually by becoming defensive. On the other hand, she may cop to what she's doing. Or she could make a case that completely justifies her behavior. Either way, listen to what she has to say and tell her you hope the two of you can work things out.

# FRONT ROW

**mission:**

**To get great seats without doing anything stupidly expensive or scuzzy.**

Whether it's a U2 concert or a Lakers game, one thing's for sure—it's a lot harder these days to score the Sweet Seats. Security is tighter and tickets are beyond the budget of anyone without a trust fund. That's why, like so many other things in life, getting a good seat has everything to do with who you know.

Hence, these few simple tips for getting tickets. It's a dirty job, but somebody's gotta do it.

## Tactical Maneuvers
### SHOP THE BOX OFFICE

Always shop the box office before you hit TicketMaster. With TM, you'll be suckered for all kinds of "service" charges that'll send your $15 ticket price to the shy side of $30 in no time. Also, the box office will sometimes release extra tickets the day of the show.

## SHOW UP THE SAME DAY AS THE BIG EVENT

For most major shows, there is almost always someone

* whose date didn't show up,

* who is a member of the press and has an extra ticket, or

* who won tickets on the radio and had to go alone.

Your chances for scoring this free ticket are always better when you're alone (although sometimes there is strength in numbers—two of you can work opposite ends of the venue).

## CALL THE BROKER

If you must be in the front row of the show, try a ticket broker. Find a reputable one through the National Association of Ticket Brokers (www.natb.org). Or shop around with local brokers, since they usually have long-term contracts with nearby venues. Just don't be a total sucker—call at least three brokers, since prices will vary.

## TRY THE RADIO

Listen to your favorite local radio station to win tickets.

## LAST POSSIBLE RESORT

Learn how to write reviews (free is OK, but paying is better) for a weekly newspaper, Web site, magazine, whatever, and score tickets through your press contacts. This routine has kept many a poorly paid freelance writer from seriously hating life.

## THE INTERMISSION SCAM

This is a sneaky way to see a big show—or, at least, half of one—for free. Here's the drill: Turn up for the show after it begins, then, when everyone comes out at intermission, mingle with the crowd. Walk back inside the theater with the crowd when they return to the seats. Now find some empty seats to plop down in—ushers almost never check tickets on the way back! This trick works for operas, ballets, and other upscale events, too. Just be sure to wear your fancy duds, not your torn jeans, so you fit in with the swells.

One caveat: This scam is not for the ethically squeamish or the easily embarrassed. Technically, it's illegal. While you're not likely to be thrown in jail if you're caught, you will probably be thrown out of the theater.

# GREASE THE PALM

**mission:**
**To learn the subtle art of persuasive payola.**

When a customer eats a meal in a restaurant, she *tips* the server when paying the bill. When she signs up for cable and decides she wants all the premium channels for the low, low price of free, she *bribes* the cable guy. Tipping requires common sense, but bribing requires real style.

## Tipping Tactics

The following tips are the minimum you should leave in various situations. If your server has really gone above and beyond, let your conscience be your guide. *Note: Rules for tipping in other countries may differ. Always check before you assume.*

### ALWAYS TIP THE:
• Waiter, waitress, and headwaiter: Serving people in a restaurant is a hellish

job and one that most of us have endured. We recommend you always tip 20%, unless the service is lousy (defined by completely forgetting your order, as opposed to bringing you the wrong wine); then you can tip 10%. But never stiff your waiter completely—these people survive on their tips.

The point here is that **it doesn't cost much to be generous.** Will it really kill you to give a buck or two to the lady in the bathroom?

- Bartender and wine steward: 15%
- Checkroom attendant: $1 per coat, or $2 for extra stuff like packages, umbrellas, briefcases, etc.
- Washroom attendant: 50¢–$2, depending on the service they provide.
- Strolling musicians in restaurants: $1 a song per musician (three songs played by three musicians would cost you $9).
- Valet: $2.
- Hotel doorman: $1–$2 if they give your bags to the bellman; $1–$3 for summoning a taxi; $1–$2 for bringing your car to the door.
- Hotel bellman: $1 per bag, especially if they bring it to your room.
- Hotel maid: $2 per night per person in large hotel; $1 per night per person in small hotel. Leave in an envelope that says "Housekeeping" if you can't find him or her in person.
- Room-service waiter: Tip just like any other waiter.
- Concierge: $5 minimum for handling airline or theater reservations; $10 if they go above and beyond the call of duty (like getting you tickets to Siegfried & Roy).
- Skycap: $1 per bag.
- Taxi driver: 20% of the fare; more if they go out of their way for you (e.g., carrying your bags to your front door).
- Hair colorist, masseuse or masseur, hairstylist, aromatherapist, facialist, makeup artist, aesthetician, nail technician: 15-20% of the fee.
- Shampoo person: $1–$3.
- Car-washer: $2–$3.

- Garage attendant: $1.
- Grocery loader: $1–$2, depending on the number of bags he or she takes to your car and loads.
- Cleaning staff, baby-sitter: Holiday tips of $10-$25 and a personal gift.

## The Basics of Bribing

Good for siblings, cable guys, some employees in foreign countries, and the occasional ex-lover.

When traveling, carry lots of ones. Cash a twenty before you even head to the airport, and, voilà, there's your tip fund. Take note of this travel advice from a particularly savvy (just slightly pampered) Traveler: **"Never carry anything heavier than a dollar bill."**

1. Never, ever offer money to a cop. This is illegal and could land you in jail. Can you say "slammer" en Español?

2. Bribing requires the keen skills of a good listener. If the potential bribee is trying to resolve a situation, wait until there's an opening in the conversation; then ask if there's a quicker or more efficient way to work out the situation.

3. Only offer what you can afford to pay (i.e., don't tell your sister you'll loan her your Anna Sui sweater if it actually belongs to your best friend).

4. Never say this: "If I give you five bucks, will you let me cut to the front of the line?" Try this instead: "This is a really long line, and I have to get back to work before my boss fires me. Would ten dollars move me any closer to the front?"

5. And don't forget: Payola comes in many forms besides cold cash—sometimes favors, goods, or services make excellent bribes.

### Bribing Your Friends

If you ask your friends to do you a big favor (like paint your apartment), they deserve a reward. Tell them you'll buy pizzas and beer. **Tip: Never offer something and then fail to deliver.** Talk is cheap, and you will be, too!

You're Invited!

List of friends
Bill
Eric
Sue
Irq
Paula
Jose
Brian
Lilly
Stan
Gail
Niles
Phil
Chester

Guest List o' Plenty

Innovative Blender Cocktails

MADONNA music

← Hot ← Tunes

JANET JACKSON
DMX
JILL SCOTT
BJORK
MOBY
REM

Loungy Pillows →

faboo appetizers →

← sushi

← shrimp

← olives

FIGUIER

candles & scents

# GROOVEABLE FEAST

## mission:

**To throw a bash where no one gets arrested, or a dinner party where no one gets a) bored or b) food poisoning.**

Of course, we know you know how to party. But we're talking about more than another debauched night on the town. We're talking about your skills at throwing a semi-grown-up soiree—the kind without a keg or police intervention. A smashing party is the mark of a true adult—a real coming-of-age ritual that can win you friends, clients, and a few interesting new phone numbers.

A successful fete can be broken down into three simple components:

1. Guests
2. Ambience
3. Food and Drink

Let's review them all.

## Guests

FOR THE BLOWOUT: The trick to a blowout is volume, so invite everyone you know, and tell them the more the merrier. More importantly—invite your neighbors. If they don't come, the cops probably will later.

FOR THE INTIMATE GATHERING. Invite people who will work together socially. Think of people who might be interesting to one another but who aren't too much alike. So if all your friends are actors, we're sorry. Just kidding. Be sure to invite at least a couple of guests who have more to talk about than their last audition rejection.

FOR THE DINNER PARTY: Don't seat the rabid atheist next to the pious Catholic, unless you like the idea of food fights around your table.

## Ambience

Music is key. Always have a great selection of tunes (CDs or mix tapes) playing. *Never* play the radio. There's nothing worse than hearing ads blasting over cocktail conversation.

Set the mood with lighting. The best party-givers despise naked lightbulbs. Cover yours with paper Chinese balloons or Indian/Tibetan folding screens. String little white strands of Xmas lights or kitsch ones (like chili peppers or animals) over doorways. Put candles everywhere (yummy ones made with essential oil are great but keep them far from where people are eating). Tiki torches set a perfect tropical mood for outdoor parties.

Scent is seductive and instantly arouses good vibes in your guests. Burn incense (not too sweet but interesting, like Black Love or Nag Champa). Place sweet-smelling flowers (like lilies, narcissus, roses) around in small bunches.

Your seating set-up often determines the mood of a party. Big, comfy pillows give a loungy feel to your room. Lots of chairs tell people you expect it to be a mellow gathering. And of course, clear a big space for dancing if you want people to boogie down.

## Food and Drink

Keep the drinks flowing. Whether you're juicin' 40s or sipping sparkling cider, there should always be enough to drink. Tip: Make sure you have two blenders for dueling margaritas.

### Grooveable Feast Tip #2

A party should always be a little disorderly. Hook dissimilar people up and steer them toward things in common they can chat about (they both love gangster movies or are passionate about indie bands). If someone is sitting solo, ask him if he'd like a drink or try to draw him into conversation with someone else. That's the mark of a truly smooth hostess.

Where there is drink, there should always be food. Nibbles include salty snacks (like olives or nuts), chicken wings, chips and salsa, shrimp cocktail, hummus and pitas, and cheese and crackers. With all due respect to Martha, making a gazillion different appetizers is way too time-consuming. If you live near a Trader Joe's or a Costco, they sell great assortments of frozen hors d'oeuvres.

It's always fun to introduce a drink du jour. Hence the Love Grenade. It'll have them lining up. Fill a blender about halfway with ice cubes. Then add one part Southern Comfort and two parts orange juice. Blend, then pour into glasses. Float a splash of Grand Marnier on top, then light it. (Make sure to use a long lighter-wand.)

faboo *petizers

← Sushi

← shrimp

← olives

If you are cooking for your shindig, don't get too complicated. On a date, for example, don't serve student food (spaghetti with tomato sauce), but don't bust out the paté, either. Make a dish you feel confident cooking. Or get your guests to help you cook. *Note: This is a gamble, since there are some guests who like to watch, rather than cook.*

**65**

| The Occasion | The Music |
|---|---|
| **Big Bash/Shake Your Booty** | Everyone loves disco; mix current music with oldies (like Moby with the *Carwash* sound track). Or play the music that makes your group nostalgic. It could be '80s tunes (Blondie, The Smiths, Bauhaus, New Order), late '70s punk rock (The Ramones, Sex Pistols, The Clash), or old-school hip-hop (Grandmaster Flash, Whodini, Roxanne Shante). |
| **Small Sit-Down Dinner Party** | You want the evening to have an **Eclectic & Mellow** sultry groove (Miles Davis, Cesaria Evora, Buena Vista Social Club, Nightmares on Wax, Thievery Corporation, Massive Attack, Bebel Gilberto). |
| **A Date/Getting to Know You** | The music should reflect who you are without being intrusive (Serge Gainsbourg—especially with Brigitte Bardot—vintage Dolly Parton, Spain, Chet Baker, etc.). |
| **Booty Call/Butt Naked** | Whatever gets your motor running (D'Angelo)! |

Don't leave your antique heirloom diamond necklace lying out. **Hide all your valuables**, and put breakables someplace safe. Why tempt fate or the infrequent sticky-fingered party guest?

## How to Create a Boomin' Buffet

* In terms of decor, think big (bowls, baskets, large quantities of food) and bold colors (like red, black, and gold for a Chinese-themed table). Go to town on decorations when it comes to your buffet.

* Always have a focal point for the buffet. It doesn't have to be a fussy centerpiece. Try an overflowing

basket (filled with some-thing that sets a theme) at the end of the table.

\* A table filled with flat trays and small food doesn't look like much. Arrange food at various heights and angles to give the table some drama.

## *Grooveable Feast Tip #3*

If you decide to throw the kind of bash where people can't remember what they did, make sure you provide cab numbers and that there are designated drivers when people leave. And it might be easier to do this if you stay sober, too. Sorry.

## Bonus Party Advice—the Flip Side
### HOW TO GET OUT OF A LAME PARTY

There's nothing worse than getting dressed up for a night out on the town only to get to your fabulous fete and find out it's a funeral in disguise. When you find it necessary to cut out right after you've arrived, relax. Have a drink (free booze!), then find your host or hostess and explain that a) you have cramps or b) you have to get up early tomorrow morning or c) you had a really long day and are exhausted. Then beat it.

Hostess jitters are as common as late guests. Don't stress. Your job is to welcome people and **enjoy the fun**.

## *Grooveable Feast Tip #4*

Get creative when you set your dinner table. Forget the centerpiece and do a low row of potted miniature roses instead. Or put interesting objects—like rocks, candles, and two-sided photo frames—on the table. Use fake fur, Astroturf, or vinyl for funky placemats. Mix up patterns for napkins, and use twigs or lemongrass tied in knots for napkin holders.

# HIGHWAY TO HELL

**mission:**
**To keep your driving rap sheet short and sweet.**

There's something about getting behind the wheel that makes us all giddy inside. It's a car thing. It's a freedom thing. How else are we supposed to tail people? On foot? In platforms? Ha!

## Driving Maneuvers Your High School Teacher Never Told You About

### THE DUI BLUES

Driving after you've been drinking goes against the rule of smart babes everywhere. In case you're unclear on this point, let's review it in big, bold letters: Real women DO NOT drink and drive. Sure, there's a difference between having one cocktail and having four, but here's a reality check— you are considered legally impaired long before you actually feel drunk. So don't be stupid. If you drink, call a cab or hitch a ride with a friend.

Do you know the clues to help you size up this situation?

Never, ever drive with empties in your car. If a cop spots them, he automatically has reason to search your car and give you a sobriety test.

**BAD SCENARIO:**

It's Gail's birthday, and after two hours of partying after work, she leaves the Kasbah to drive home in her '69 Chevy Camaro. Gail figures since she only had one glass of champagne and three Cosmopolitans, she's okay to drive. Problem is, she also had a fight with her boyfriend, Raffi, so Gail's really not paying a lot of attention to the road. After straddling the lane while lighting a cigarette, weaving while trying to find decent music on the radio, and taking an extra-wide turn*, she hears the unmistakable sound of a police siren right behind her. Gail pulls over and waits for Officer Big Stick to approach her.

Gail has obviously never thought twice about a little something called blood alcohol content (BAC). It stands for the amount of alcohol that's found in your bloodstream, and cops measure it to determine whether you're over the legal limit (which varies from state to state). In most states, you are considered legally drunk when your BAC is .08 (that's 8%) or higher. Problem is, no one wants to go to the trouble of calculating his or her BAC while standing at the Tiki bar.

*Cops are on the lookout for drunk drivers, and sloppy moves like a wide turn tip them off that you are three sheets to the wind.

So here's a rule of thumb: If you're driving, never drink more than one drink per hour, and never more than three drinks in one outing. (If you're smaller than average—less than 120 pounds—your limit should really be two drinks.)

To be more conservative, alternate your drinks: one beer, then a soft drink, etc. To understand how BAC works, let's take Gail as an example. She weighs 130 pounds and had four drinks—probably very strong drinks, too. (Cosmos are usually on the boozy side.) In other words, Gail's in trouble.

## CUI—Crying Under the Influence

Avoid drinking + driving + crying. It's a fact that the effects of alcohol are intensified when you are in an emotional state. We've heard of an Operative in the middle of a breakup who puked all night after drinking one beer. When you're freaking out, drown your sorrows at home, or even better, down a soothing, hot drink (superrich hot chocolate with fat marshmallows can hit the spot).

Gail's about to face The Man. What should she do?

* First, she should pop an Altoids in her mouth. It's not proven, but there's a strong rumor that these powerhouse mints not only help cover up the smell of alcohol on your breath but can screw up the Breathalyzer results, too.

* Deny, deny, deny. Under no circumstances should Gail tell Officer Big Stick that she's been drinking. He will not care if she's had only one drink, and any admission of imbibing will give him more reason to make Gail walk the line.

* If Gail is a good liar, she should have a story ready about where she really was. ("Officer, I've been at work since six this morning and am just now going home. I'm exhausted.")

* In some states, you can object to taking a Breathalyzer test, request the one you want to take, or respectfully request to have an attorney present before you answer any questions. In other states, you can't.

One more time: Don't drive after drinking.

> ### Highway Patrol Tip #2
> Do not behave like people on Cops if you get pulled over. Always be courteous and respectful (in other words, bite your tongue), and have your driver's license and registration in a handy spot.

71

## Speeding Tickets

Until you're having fun, fun, fun on the Autobahn, you have to drive slow, slow, slow in the States. That doesn't mean you should crawl at 55 miles per hour when everyone else is cruising at 70. That's just a good way to get flipped the bird by your friendly fellow drivers. Keeping up with the speed of traffic is key and usually safer. (Slow cars sometimes actually cause accidents.) In general, you can drive 5 to 8 miles per hour over the speed limit on highways. On streets, don't go more than 5 over the limit if you want to stay out of speeding ticket school. And never speed in a school zone—that will get you in real trouble, not to mention brand you a real jerk.

### Ticket Tactics

1. When speeding, keep in mind that if you are pulled over and the cop finds you were sailing by at 15 miles per hour above the speeding limit, you'll get hit with major fines and insurance hikes. So if you were speeding at 70 miles per hour in a 55 miles per hour zone, try to talk the cop down a mile. A ticket stating you were only 14 miles per hour over the speeding limit will keep you on this side of the "Dangerous Driver" line.
2. Ditch the Police Union decal. You should support the police because you want to, not

because you think it'll save you from a speeding ticket. A bumper sticker never saved anyone from getting busted.

3. Down South they call it "pork bait." OK, it's a terrible name, but it describes those folks who fly past everyone else. If you speed, set your cruise control to go slower than the PB who's just rocketed past you at 80 mph. Hopefully, that guy will be the one who gets pulled over instead of you.

4. In some areas, there are posted signs stating that the speed limit is enforced by aircraft. We've never known anyone to get a ticket from a cop in an airplane. Use your own discretion.

## Highway Patrol Tip #5

If you speed past a cop and your eyes meet, give a friendly nod and carefully but quickly step on the brakes. This way, you're letting him know you're trying to correct the "situation." If he decides to pursue you, pull over immediately. Cops don't like to chase anyone, and an irate cop means hard times for you.

# HIT THE ROAD

**mission:**

To be fully prepared for a break for the border (or for the closest mai-tai-soaked resort town) at all times.

If you're the traveling-adventuress type, this section was written for you. We know your wanderlusting kind—you live for new countries, new experiences, and new, non-English-speaking hotties. While others sit and daydream, you're booking the next getaway to an exotic beach, wild safari, or road trip to the next town with a day spa. To make your travel fantasy come true (except for the part about that surfer guy), you need only two things: a See Ya Sucker Stash and a properly packed Bug-Out Bag. Remember: With careful planning, you, too, could spend that summer in Greece with just a bathing suit bottom and a few good books. Okay, a few trashy books.

## See Ya Sucker Stash

Want to know the biggest obstacle between you and that life-changing trip to Belize? Here's a hint: It's not finding someone to go with or getting the time off work. Nope, as is true for so many things in life, it's *cash*—the cold hard stuff—and lots of it. Consider this:

## Pricey vs. Priceless

A pair of Jimmy Choo shoes vs. airfare to France

An expensive dinner at Le Swanque Café vs. a week's worth of meals on the beach in Sri Lanka

A new work outfit (yawn!) vs. a few nights in a sleepy seaside town in Mexico

An annual gym membership (double yawn!) vs. a monthlong trek through Nepal

So go to your bank, open a brand-spanking-new savings account, and call it the See Ya Sucker Stash. Then make a point of putting some cash in it every week. The amount can be a little ($20) or a lot. Keep your savings book in a plastic bag, along with colorful travel brochures to your dream destinations, and stick it in the deep freeze (the refrigerator). Take it out only to register your deposits or when you're ready to take a trip. But that's all you're allowed to take it out for. Period. No ifs, ands, or buts. Got it? Good.

**Note:** We know of a traveling girl who keeps at least five changes of clothes in the trunk of her car. Do not turn into this person. **Sometimes too much preparedness is a bad thing.**

# The Bug-Out Bag

One of the marks of a superior traveler is adaptability. And for maximum adaptability, we recommend you go out and get yourself a Bug-Out Bag. The BOB is like your purse, but better. It's the first thing you grab when you've gotta hit the road fast.

## 10 Essential Items for a Bug-Out Bag

The rest is up to you!

1. Lavender oil. Good for cuts, a stress-relieving bath, a peaceful sleep, or masking the smell of a rank gas-station bathroom.

2. A journal and pencil with sharpener. It's important to stoke your creativity and an awareness of your surroundings.
3. Unlubed condoms. For obvious reasons, but also when placed inside a sock, they can hold up to a liter of water.
4. Small tube of lube. Also for obvious reasons.

5. Dried fruit, like apricots or bananas, and Luna bars. Especially useful for quick energy boosts and in airports where the food is more dangerous than any "mechanical problem."
6. Slouchy hat and stylin' sunglasses. For a quick, low-key (not to mention wildly fashionable) disguise.

7. A Swiss Army knife with a beer/wine bottle opener, can opener, nail file, scissors, and tweezers.
8. Favorite paperback that you don't mind rereading.
9. Mini-makeup bag. It should contain tinted lip balm; sunscreen with 15 SPF; mascara; soothing eye gel; and triple-duty lipstick in a shade that works for lips, cheeks, and eyes (for when you need to change your identity fast).

10. Tissue packs. Wipe your butt, hands, nose, mouth, whatever. . . .

# The Ultimate Globetrotter's Book List

For some of us, it's Jackie Collins or bust. But when you're hankering for something with a wandering theme, check out one of the following books:

*Desert Places* or *Tracks* by Robyn Davidson
Robyn kicks ass! Walking 1,700 miles across the Australian desert with only four camels and her dog for company and crossing the desert in India. She writes about it all—and herself—candidly, no matter how ugly it gets.

*On the Road* by Jack Kerouac
Okay, begrudgingly listed since the gals in it go nowhere. Despite this, it's damn good. A cross-country hitchhiking tale that some say has changed their lives.

*Maiden Voyage* by Tania Aebi
Your basic barfly-turned-world-traveler story. Tania's life changed when her dad offered her a college education or a 26-foot sailing ship. Duh! She sailed around the world by herself for two and a half years— and she was only 18.

*West with the Night* by Beryl Markham
This spectacular memoir is based on Beryl's life in Kenya, where she became an African bush pilot and the first person to fly solo across the Atlantic from east to west.

*The Teachings of Don Juan: A Yaqui Way of Knowledge* by Carlos Castaneda
OK, so it's a little out there for a travel book. Just think of it as a different kind of trip.

*Out of Africa* by Isak Dinesen
A love story between a Danish aristocrat and Kenya—not Robert Redford. Great writing, and miles better than the hokey movie.

*Islands in the Clouds* by Isabella Tree
A very cool story about Isabella's journeys to the remote Highlands of Papua New Guinea and Irian Jaya—one of the most dangerous regions on Earth.

*The Beach* by Alex Garland
A boy-style thriller set in Thailand.

*Travels with Charley: In Search of America* by John Steinbeck
A camper, a poodle, and an amazing writer travel across America circa 1960. A lovely read, with many observations still poignantly true today—like those about rampant tourism. If he only knew. Great dog writing, too.

*Drive: Women's True Stories from the Open Road* Edited by Jeannie Goode
These refreshing essays come from women, young and old. What unites them? The open road, girl, where they find many adventures and do a little inner tripping to boot.

# HOME FOR THE HOLIDAYS

**mission:**
**To survive your next family reunion without**
**anybody getting hurt and/or disowned**

It's a fact of life that the longer you're away from your family, the more you imagine how fun it is to spend time with them (conveniently forgetting the last 26 painful occasions). The dream: a cozy holiday get-together with your loved ones. The reality: Dad planted in front of a blaring TV. Your sibs squabbling over some childhood grievance, then turning on anyone who tries to intervene. Mom refusing to come out of her bedroom. Old Uncle Marv telling that story about the saucy Italian honey he romanced during WWII. Aunt Pearl "accidentally" dropping her hot tea in Uncle Marv's lap. And you bolting to your car for a quick getaway.

Sound familiar? We thought so. Don't despair—consider these temper-saving tips before blowing up over the Thanksgiving turkey.

## The Tactics

No matter how your family treats you, you are in control of your own reactions. That's right, nobody is making you fling the turkey at your brother-in-law's fat head. Furthermore, your sister doesn't make you wish she'd never been born; rather, you are choosing to have this nasty (albeit satisfying) thought all on your own. Once you realize that you are in charge of your emotions, you'll start to look twice at the stuff that really chaps your butt (a psychological term).

* Notions of right and wrong have no place in family politics. If you focus on what's fair, you'll be bitter for the rest of your life. So what if you spent two years of your teenage life grounded while your bratty kid brother partied until daybreak? Let it go. (Besides, you can always make up for lost time.)

* Be realistic about your expectations of other people. Is it fair—or realistic— to expect your grandma to appreciate the fine workmanship behind your latest tattoo?

### What to Do When Good Parents Go Bad

If your parents say things that hurt your feelings, remember that their thoughtless behavior is something they learned, probably from another relative. Try to keep that reality check in mind before you lash out with a nasty comeback. Your grown-up behaviour may help them a) realize that they're being dolts and b) want to change. *Note: If they are abusive or physically harmful, do not subject yourself to their behavior. Get out and stay away until they've changed.*

## Three Clues to Keeping Your Cool

Consider these things when talking with a family member, or anyone else for that matter.

## Home for the Holidays Tip #2

Be sure to ask your older relatives questions about family history. It makes them feel good and has the added value of giving you excellent dirt on other relatives, especially your parents. This also gets high ratings for entertainment value at family functions.

* Don't yell. Your point will come across stronger if you speak in a normal tone. Yelling is ineffective anyway. (Yes, even when your Rush-Limbaugh-lovin' dad tells you that vegetarians are ruining the world.) It only brings real communication to a screeching stop. If you really disagree, change the subject.

* Perfect your timing. Learn to speak at the proper time, not when it's best for you.

* And no name-calling, either. You won't persuade anyone to see your side of the argument by getting personal. We know it is tempting to fall back on "Oh yeah, well, you're fat!" from time to time. (It's a classic!) But chances are it won't make your sister see your point about the defense budget.

## Home for the Holidays Tip #3

If you let go of those nastier feelings you've got lurking inside—anger, hurt, resentment, and jealousy are the biggies—your world will be a much happier place, we promise. C'mon, are you really still peeved about your older sister selling your bike in fourth grade?

## Home for the Holidays Tip #4

Get this into your stubborn head: There's no such thing as a "perfect" family. Ozzie and Harriet had a few knock-down-drag-outs, too. Accept your family members for who they are—not who you want them to be.

No name calling!

# HOME REMEDY

**mission:**

**To cure your body and create kitchen concoctions that would make Martha buy stock in YOUR company.**

A good Operative is never sloppy in her professional—or personal—habits. It's all in the details. Yes, we mean personal hygiene. Picture La Femme Nikita in her stilettos, training her telescopic lens on an unsuspecting target and letting out a huge belch. It just isn't a very compelling image.

## Bad Breath

In high school, we had a teacher who midlecture would swig on a bottle of Listerine, walk to the window, open it, and spit. Yes, the dude was a freak. Even worse, his breath still stank. Guys like this you expect it from, but bad breath could never happen to you, right? *Right.* Read on, and learn how to battle your own bodacious breath.

## THE CULPRITS

1. Stinky foods. Anchovies, garlic, blue cheese, pepperoni, salami, onions—yup, all that good stuff will make you reek.

2. Dry mouth. Medication, illness—like a cold, infection, upset stomach, or sinusitis—and dehydration can all cause dry mouth and give yours that funky taste and smell.

3. Dental drama. Gum disease and plaque are two very obvious culprits behind el stinko breatho.

4. Too much partying. Alcohol, tobacco, and drugs. Pucker up!

5. Menstrual cycle. Swelling gums = stinky breath.

6. Dieting or fasting. When you diet, your body breaks down stored fat and protein for fuel, all of which can add up to a scary breath situation.

## THE CURE

1. Obviously, the quickest way to discover the source of your bad breath is to go to a dentist to make sure you don't have something lurking in your mouth.

2. If the dentist gives you the all-clear, adjust your diet, drink lots of water, and brush your teeth—and tongue—at least twice a day. Tip: Brushing your tongue, as well as your teeth, reduces mouth odor by 85%. You remove bacterial plaque, food debris, and dead cells.

3. Floss every day, without fail.

4. Forget alcohol-based mouth-wash. Alcohol dries out your mouth tissues and causes them to secrete pungent plasma proteins. (Mmm, sweet, huh?) Instead, use a chloro-phyll-based mouthwash (available at most health food stores).

5. Chewing parsley, anise, ten-nel, or cloves after meals can also do the trick. Or try this bad-breath-busting potion: Mix 3 drops of peppermint oil, 1/2 cup of aloe vera juice, and 1/2 teaspoon of vegetable glycerin in a glass bottle. Shake well, and gargle whenever you think your breath is smelly. Tip: You can store this for up to a week as long as you keep it covered in a cool, dark place.

*Home Remedy Tip #2*

You could have bad breath and not know it. Blame it on science; specifically, a creepy phenomenon called adaptation. It means we get used to our own smells—scary! To find out if you have bad breath, ask a friend. If you'd rather not gross her out, try a self-test: Lick your wrist, wait 30 seconds, and smell. Whew!

## Burping/Farting (It's a gas thing.)

Some gals get it when they're nervous; others when they've eaten too many beans. In turn-of-the-century France, a deadpan man named Pujol became very wealthy scandalizing and entertaining audiences with his master blaster act (only in France . . .).

### THE CULPRITS

1. Swallowing air. Sure, we all breathe air, but when you eat or drink too fast, you will "come up" for air in between. So don't be a pig.

2. The breakdown of undigested foods. It's just like your mother always said: Take the time to let your food digest. Slow down, and don't jump up from the table right away.

Gas can also be a result of food allergies or a stomach-related issue. See a doctor if relief doesn't come after taking The Cure or if you are in constant pain.

## THE CURE

1. Since swallowing air is the most common cause of gas, don't gobble your food or drinks (sometimes a problem for girls on the go). Chew slowly with your mouth closed. Sometimes breathing deeply for a minute before you start eating can help you relax while you chew.

2. Avoid carbonated drinks, chewing gum, and airy foods (whipped cream, soufflés). It makes sense when you think about it: The more air you take in, the more you'll let out.

3. Remember that farting is unavoidable. Apparently, it's normal to pass gas 14 to 23 times a day. (Turns out that excuse your ex used to give was true.) And as you've probably figured out, sometimes it stinks, sometimes it don't. It is also a supremely unfair fact that a healthy diet can cause a "gaseous situation." So if your diet is filled with stuff like dairy products, beans, fruits, vegetables, and whole grains, then good for you—but consider yourself warned.

4. Try this natural remedy for gas: Put a teaspoon of caraway seeds in a pan, cover with water, boil, and simmer for 10 minutes. Let your concoction cool, and sip it slowly before you eat. Alternatively, you could chew a few caraway seeds after a meal, drink a glass of warm water, and breathe deeply for 10 minutes.

5. Sip peppermint (for digestion) or chamomile (calming) tea after dinner.

6. Eat frequent small meals rather than three large ones.

7. To relax your esophagus muscles (and allow trapped gas to escape), put a drop of peppermint, ginger, or cinnamon extract (available at the health food store) in a cup of water, and sip it after a meal.

# Yeast Infections

This is the most delicate of hygiene issues as well as the subject of countless moronic TV commercials. ("Sally, are you plagued by intimate itching?") The lowdown: Yeast infections are caused by an overgrowth of candida albicans, a fungus usually found in small quantities in the vaginal and intestinal tracts.

*Home Remedy Tip #4*

Only try these remedies if you are sure you have a yeast infection. If you are unsure, or if the symptoms are recurring, get your lover checked and talk to your gynecologist. These could be symptoms of a larger problem.

### THE SYMPTOMS

    1. A thick, white vaginal discharge with no odor.

    2. A white coating of the vagina.

### THE CULPRITS

    1. Antibiotics. They kill bad and good bacteria.

    2. Tight pants. Apologies to all the cha-cha's out there.

    3. Hot bubble baths. We love 'em, but they don't always love us.

    4. Nylon panties and pantyhose. Cotton panties and stockings are sexier anyway.

    5. Feminine deodorant sprays and douches. These are just wrong. The chemicals in them can irritate your vagina as well as destroy its pH balance—learn to love your scent!

    6. Hormones. Like those found in the Pill.

**Fact:** Men with yeast infections (yeah, they get 'em, too) may have an irritated and red penis or scrotum. Cute.

Cool Baths!

← cotton panties

7. Doing It. Unfortunately, yeast infections can be sexually transmitted.

8. A weakened immune system. Illness can cause yeast infections.

9. Too much sugar. Not only does the sweet stuff mess with your moods, but it also upsets your pH balance.

## THE CURE

Over-the-counter methods cost a lot, and your body can become resistant to them. These natural remedies bring relief and are a lot cheaper.

1. Take nondairy acidophilus (healthy bacteria) capsules orally, or insert them into your vagina.

2. Eat lots of yogurt. Or better yet, take plastic tampon applicators and fill them with unsweetened, plain yogurt. Stick 'em in the freezer (or don't), and pop them into your vagina at night when you have an infection. The coolness will feel great and help to relieve that burning yeastie. Tip: Be sure to wear a pad when you do this.

3. Being constipated can sometimes cause yeast infections. You've gotta get regular. Eat apples, prunes, or figs. Drink lots of water and exercise.

4. Apple cider vinegar douches are very potent. They help establish the proper pH in your vagina. Once a day, add 1 tablespoon of vinegar to 1 quart of water, pour it in your douche kit (available at drugstores), lie down in the tub, and go to it. This is really effective when used in combination with yogurt suppositories.

5. Didn't you know? Garlic suppositories are the latest rage. Unwrap a clove and insert it into your vagina at night. Take it out in the morning. *Note: If you're allergic to garlic, don't try this cure. Ouch.*

6. Drink unsweetened cranberry juice.

7. Boric acid suppositories sound

For Yeast Infections

apples

yogurt

prunes

scary, but those in the know swear by them. Buy empty capsules (size 0) and boric acid powder (available at the pharmacy). Fill up a capsule and insert one deeply into your vagina each morning and evening for three to seven days. If you have chronic yeast infections, continue for two to four more weeks.

# J.O.B. BLUES

**mission:**

**To land that dream job, or at least manage
the crappy one without going postal.**

In a fair world, the job market would be a happy place.
It would be one in which employers were tickled pink to find you, a wildly
talented employee, and would scramble to give you a fat salary and fatter
expense account in exchange for the privilege of seeing you five days a
week. And in that same fair world, unemployment would be a time for
lounging—not scrounging. But we all know the bitter truth: Sometimes
the job market is a scary place where employers turn a blind eye to your
finer creative talents and the sky-high salary they justify. And if you're
unemployed, instead of enjoying your time off from the nine-to-five
world, you'll actually spend it worrying about how far you can stretch
that last measly paycheck and feeling lonely because all of your friends
are at work. The solution? Find new jobless (whoops, freelance) friends
or . . . get a job.

## Pounding the Pavement: Landing a Paycheck

* Figure out what you want to do. Don't know? Figure out what you like to do. Think about your skills, personality traits, and favorite hobbies. But contemplate what floats your boat and what you require from a job. A feeling of integrity? (Try working for a nonprofit.) Night hours? (Performance artist.) The opportunity to yell at people? (Movie producer or the stock exchange.) Whatever it is, brainstorm and write it all down. Then read it through, do some research, and make a list of your top five dream jobs.

* Create a short but sweet résumé. Bluffing is sometimes OK in person (like if you've never waited tables but know you could pull it off), but *never* do it on paper.

* Get a sharp, well-groomed job-hunting ensemble together. **Job-Hunting Fashion Don'ts:** Lace, cleavage, midriff-baring ensembles, chipped nail polish, heavily lacquered hair, stilettos (passé), Lycra dresses, chewing gum, heroin chic (so passé).

* Check the newspaper for jobs or cold-call companies. (This really works! See Tip #2.) Networking is the ultimate job-hunting strategy—once again, it's all about who you know. If you can get somebody to recommend you, it will make the difference between your résumé landing in Human Resources Wasteland (the best way *not* to get hired) and on your future boss's desk.

* Make a great impression on the interview. Research the job or company

before you go in so that you can talk about it coherently. ("So what does this company do again?" will not make a good impression.) Have a firm handshake. Stand up straight, sit up straighter. Don't fidget. Be sincere. Speak clearly. And always send a short thank-you note after the interview.

### J.O.B. Blues Tip#3

Temping is an excellent shortcut to landing a permanent job in a place where you really want to work. Call and ask which temp agencies your target company uses most. Then set up an appointment with the agency. Bonus: Temps are rarely given much responsibility, so you can scope out the company while getting paid for it.

## How to Survive a Bad Job
### (see also: Boss from Hell)

1. Take walks at lunchtime. Exercise helps clear the head and relieves you of any homicidal tendencies you may have suddenly developed.
2. As much as you may want to, do not develop the self-destructive habit of complaining about coworkers. It always comes around to haunt you and always makes you look like a jerk, no matter how right you are. Instead, think of it as an opportunity to gather material for that book you plan to write about demented department heads someday.
3. Start looking for a new job. (Duh.) But be sneaky about it. You don't want word to leak out before you're ready to get out of Dodge.
4. Try to get laid off. That way you can collect unemployment while you job hunt.

## Useful Things You Can Learn During a Really Bad Job

- How to laugh heartily at very bad jokes.
- How to make every compliment sound sincere.
- How to "borrow" office supplies.
- How to keep a straight face in any situation.
- How to fake interest in job topics while actually planning your weekend.

# KICK ASS

**mission:**
**To expect the unexpected, anticipate the worst,**
**and then kick its butt if necessary.**

Thanks to the recent Hollywood habit of making TV shows and summer flicks that feature crime-fighting, ass-kicking heroines, the phrase "hit like a girl" now has an entirely different meaning. Even better, real-life babes are also learning the joys of a well-done takedown through self-defense classes and martial arts training. If only we could all open up that can of whup-ass like Buffy. Here's what we've figured out: Fighting isn't about "muscle"—it's about speed and power, aka economy of action. Any self-defense move should be well practiced, swiftly delivered, and fully committed to (with your whole body behind it).

Remember: There are no rules. Your only goal is to escape unharmed. So don't be afraid to scream, pinch, kick, bite, hit below the belt, and generally do whatever the hell you have to do to get away.

# Basic Self-Defense Techniques

Here are just a few prime areas to hit, and how to do it:

### THE EYES AND THROAT

Curl your thumb, pinkie, and ring finger to the palm of your hand, holding the index and middle finger rigid. Strike (like a spear) straight into the eye or about a half inch above the hollow of the throat. Tip: You can also use your thumb in place of the index and middle fingers.

### THE NOSE

Spread the fingers of your hand wide and tighten your hand. On the palm-side of your larger knuckles, the area should feel very solid. With this area, strike the creep right smack in the center of the nose.

### THE FAMILY JEWELS

It's an oldie but a goodie—when in doubt, go straight for the groin. Bring your knee upward with all your force. If you can, grab the attacker's hips and pull him into the strike. Tip: Think of your knees as a point, and drive that point home!

**Using your foot,** strike your attacker with your instep. Or kick straight up and strike with your shinbone.

**Using your hand**, swing it straight up into the groin.

Being a chick gives you a fundamental advantage in a fight, because no one expects you to know how to defend yourself. So if you have a combo of some well-practiced moves (or even just one), you've got the **Surprise Factor** on your side. (As in, "Surprise! How does this feel in your man parts, creep?")

eyes

nose

throat

family jewels

Your hand should be in a fist or open, as when you strike the nose.

## THE KNEES

With all your force, drive your heel forward into the kneecap. Or strike the inside of his knee with the inside of your foot. This works best if you are standing in front of the attacker with your back to him.

If the attacker is beside you, strike hard on the inside of the knee, driving your heel sideways and downward. (You should practice this one if you want to execute it effectively.)

*Note: Maintaining your balance on knee strikes is difficult, so practice, practice, practice.*

### Kick-Ass Tip #3

All trained fighters learn to fight from **a crouch**. Contrary to popular belief, looming over your opponent is a disadvantage. If you fight from a crouch, you have greater control over your movements and better balance.

### Kick-Ass Tip #2

Sign up for a self-defense class with your posse (friends, mother, sisters). Make it a **group thing**. And remember: Just because you learn how to throw a punch doesn't mean you're compromising your girly-hood. On the contrary, only a real woman knows how to drop a punk when she has to. Watch ass-kicking movies for inspiration—we recommend anything with Michelle Yeoh (martial-arts expert extraordinaire) in it.

knees! ~

# LADY LUCK

## mission:
**To win a million dollars, buy a new wardrobe, and retire to St. Bart's— or at least look fantastic while you lose your rent money.**

## Crack the Casino Code

1. Before you make your spectacular entrance into the casino, decide how much money you're going to play with, and stick to it. (A good rule of thumb is about the price of a nice dinner.) Absolutely no visits to the ATM are allowed after you lose your original stake.

2. Never bet more than 10% of your stake. If you start chasing the cash you've lost, the odds of going broke are much higher. Only raise your bets when you're ahead.

3. Forgo the free drinks. The boozier you get, the more likely you are to throw that cash away.

4. Beware the fickle ways of Lady Luck—a slippery little wench who loves to skitter off in the middle of your winning streak. If you've won more than $100, and then lose more than $20, switch dealers. Or go eat something. Anything to get you away from the table where Lady L. has abandoned you.

# Strategies

Every gambler has her own system, good luck charms, and superstitions. Unfortunately, the odds are always in the dealer's favor, but these "rules" will, at least statistically, improve your chances.

**For stylin' inspiration,** check out *Casino* for Sharon Stone's ultimate high-roller wardrobe.

## BLACKJACK

After you've been dealt a hand, here are a few things you should remember.

### Lady Luck Tip #1

To paraphrase femme fatale Vesper Lind in *Casino Royale*, behaving like a high roller occasionally is an excellent treat. (Not to mention a chance to bust out your skintight lavender jumpsuit with the plunging neckline and a big, faux, golden fur.) Just don't turn into a freak about it. Here's a hint: If you catch yourself alone on a bus to Atlantic City with the 70+ crowd, talking excitedly about that 35 bucks you won the last time, you're in trouble. Tell the bus driver to drop you at the next Gamblers Anonymous center, pronto.

### STAND/HIT

The most basic thing to know is when to *Stand* (take no more cards) and when to *Take a Hit*. In general, you should always Stand on:
* Hard hands* of 17 and up.
* Hands of 12 through 16, if the dealer's face card is 2 through 6.
* Soft hands of 18 and up.

### THE SPLIT

A *split* is an option you have when you've been dealt two of the same card, or a pair. If you receive two 10s, for example, you can turn them both face-up, and play two hands. It's an important strategy for a good blackjack player, but you should know when to do it. Here's a quick guideline.

Always Split when:
* You get a pair of aces or 8s.
* You have any pair and the dealer's face card is 2 through 6.

* A hard hand has no ace or has an ace that must be counted as 1.

Never Split when:

* You have a pair of 4s, 5s, or 10s.

## DOUBLE DOWN

Knowing how to *Double Down* is another impor- tant part of being a suave blackjack player. It means that you double your bet midway through the game.

Here's when you should Double Down:

* On 11, unless the dealer shows an ace.
* On 10, unless the dealer shows an ace or 10.
* On 9, if the dealer shows 3 through 6.
* On soft hands* of 13 through 18, if the dealer's face card is 4 through 6.

* A soft hand has an ace that can be counted as 11 without going over 21.

## CRAPS

The unfortunately named game of craps can be complicated but it's also fun, fun, fun! Not only does it often provide the best odds, but it always seems to be where the party is on the floor. It's also an ideal game for those of us with a teensy exhi- bitionist streak, in that it offers the chance to throw dice dramatically in front of an audience of screaming strangers. *Note: Gambling + Audience = Fun.*

So even if you never understand the math-laden nuances of the game, you can learn enough of the basics to have a good time and even win a chip or two. This is a very busy game with many betting options, but here's the basic point:

Let's say you're the "shooter," or the player whose turn it is to roll the dice. You roll two normal, six-sided dice. This means the numbers you roll will add up to anything from 2 to 12. If you roll 7 or 11, you've won and the round is over. If you roll 2, 3, or 12, that's a Craps. Craps is bad. It means you've lost, or "crapped out" (we're serious!), and the round is over. If you roll any other number than the ones listed above (in other words, if you roll 4, 5, 6, 8, 9, or 10), that number becomes something called the Point.

Now your goal is to roll the dice and have them add up to the Point again. The trick is, if you roll a 7 *before* you roll the Point, you lose. So does anyone who was betting on you (so you'd better be careful about who's betting on you!). If you roll something that's neither 7 nor the point, you simply roll again until you roll either 7 or the Point. And if you roll the Point, you win. Yippee!

Here are the easiest bets to begin with:

* Pass line
* Don't pass
* Come
* Don't come (This one's fun to yell out, if nothing else.)
* "Place" bets on 6 or 8

On the first four bets, always back your bet with the "odds" bet (which increases your winnings should your number hit). Of course, this is only if you have extra money to place on the odds; otherwise, wait until you're ahead a little.

### Avoid like the plague:

Long-shot and one-roll bets, like "hardway 4."

## ROULETTE

Look glamorous sitting at the roulette table with these short and sweet tips.

Best Bets:

* "Outside" the numbers, or even-money bets (red or black; odd or even; high or low)
* If 0 or 00 comes up, you lose only half of these wagers. Other bets are lost in full.

# Casino Style

For added fun, we find the casino setting an excellent place to try out a saucy undercover ensemble. C'mon, it's the opportunity you've always wanted to see the world through cat-eye glasses, or better yet, through fake eyelashes. Here are some of our favorite ways to visit the casino incognito (also see Undercover):

**THE RETIREE.** Find anything made of man-made fibers (polyester is, of course, the classic) and be sure it's tight-fitting. Carry a plastic cup full of coins, and eat with enthusiasm at the $4 all-you-can-eat buffet. Be sure to keep that Virginia Slim burning in your ashtray at all times.

**THE ARM CANDY.** Wear something tight (boobs a-popping), tease that hair up high, and break out the sparkly eye shadow. For added effect, find a short, balding man to complete costume.

**THE CONVENTIONEER.** Slap a name badge on your corporate-casual ensemble, talk boisterously to anyone who makes eye contact with you, slap people on the back for no apparent reason.

**THE PLAYER.** (Only recommended for trust-funders.) Play games where the stakes—and the bets—are high; keep a look of intense concentration at all times; say things like "Triple down-red on the five-end." Extra points for having Arm Candy of your own.

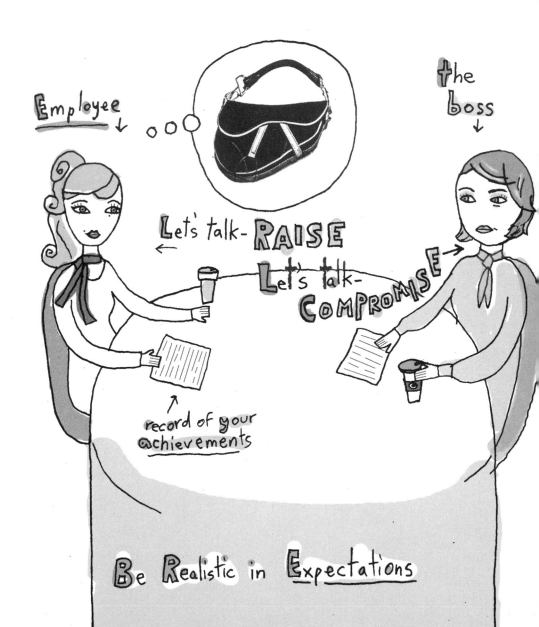

# LET'S MAKE A DEAL

## mission:
**To get what you want out of every negotiation
without putting anyone in a headlock.**

The ability to negotiate is essential to being a winner at
the game of life. In fact, this particular skill could mean the difference
between a glamorous Gucci life ("Oh well, I'll just take both pairs") and
a bargain-basement one ("Oh well, those puke-green ones are on sale,
even if they do make my feet look like gunboats"). It can also help you in
other areas of your life, like settling a tiff among the troops, pulling a fast
one on your parents, or sweet-talking your significant other into buying
you that fabulous lavender-and-hot-pink suede-and-python handbag.

## The How-To
Valerie wants a raise. She has a job that she likes—set-designing for TV
shows—but knows she should be paid more. Valerie knows her boss (let's
call her Ms. Tightwad) doesn't want to give her any more money. How
should she proceed?

## 1. BE PREPARED.

Valerie finds out everything she can about her field—most importantly, what other set designers get paid. She also checks out her competition and deduces that she is the best of the bunch at her workplace (naturally). She tries to anticipate what Ms. Tightwad might say to her, so she'll be ready for anything.

## 2. DECIDE WHAT YOU WANT, NEED, AND ARE WILLING TO SETTLE FOR.

Valerie decides that in order to survive in New York, she has to make at least $70,000 a year. She decides to shoot for the moon and ask for $90,000, figuring that Ms. Tightwad will try to lower that figure. Valerie also decides she's willing to go as low as $80,000. (That's a realistic target, since most of the people in her field make around that amount.)

*Let's Make a Deal Tip #1:*
**Fridays Off.** What if Ms. Tightwad's department really is financially strapped and a raise is out of the question? Your talks are at a standstill, and you've both decided to think on it for a day. If she's standing firm, be ready with your potential trade-offs *Note: This strategy should be used only after all other steps have failed.*

1.  You only want to work four days a week. (Use the extra day for freelance that can supplement your income.)
2.  You'd like to work from home.
3.  You'd like to bring your dog in.
4.  You'd like the use of a company car or a company cell phone.

This is your chance to use your imagination—how else can your company compensate you without taking money out of their budget?

### 3. CATCH THE BOSS IN A GOOD MOOD.

Valerie makes sure she asks Ms. Tightwad if they can meet at a time that works for both of them. Valerie knows that TW is a total freak on Fridays, since she has to review budgets. So Friday is definitely out.

### 4. ALWAYS NEGOTIATE IN PERSON.

Ms. Tightwad asks if they can talk on a day when she's out of the office. Valerie says no, because she knows that in person, she can read TW's body language and look around her office for visual cues for small talk. For example, TW has posters in her office of horses, and—guess what?—Valerie used to ride horses when she was a teenager.

### 5. NEVER NEGOTIATE WITH STRANGERS.

Ms. Tightwad then asks Valerie if she would be willing to talk with her new assistant, Mr. Small, whom Valerie has never met. She says she will fill Small in on the situation. Valerie agrees, then scopes out Small's office in advance. He has a bookshelf filled with books about WWII. Valerie's Great-uncle Pete just happened to be a highly decorated fighter pilot in WWII, and this is when all those longwinded family stories finally pay off. Our girl now knows she has something to get conversation flowing between her and Small.

### 6. ALWAYS LET THE NEGOTIATOR BRING UP THE SUBJECT AT HAND.

Valerie meets Mr. Small, they talk fighter pilots (*Thanks, Uncle Pete!*), then Valerie waits for him to bring up why she's there. She figures that she'll look too eager if she rushes into asking for more bucks. Soon, Small brings up the raise.

> *Let's Make a Deal Tip #2:*
> **What Are You Really Worth?** When evaluating your worth in the workplace on a comparative scale, consider your total contribution. Have you been there so long that it would take two people to make up for your experience? Or are your contacts so good that you save the company money on projects? Always calculate what it would cost to replace you—that's what your boss is doing during your negotiation.

## Let's Make a Deal Tip #3:

**Big Girls Don't Cry.** Or beg, or whine, or throw tantrums. One card a savvy career girl never throws is the pity card. Pity is . . . well . . . pitiful. We know it's tempting to tell your boss that your car is in the shop, you're now officially on American Express's Most Wanted list, and that you're tired of telling people that you like your apartment cold. Don't do it. It'll only make your boss uncomfortable. He might throw you a bone, but your value to him will never be the same. You want your boss to know that you're an asset—he's lucky to have you around—not a burden he has to support.

## 7. FIGURE OUT THE NEGOTIATOR'S POSITION BEFORE YOUR OWN.

Valerie waits for Mr. Small to finish telling her why he thinks she should be happy with the money she gets. He lists all the benefits of working for the company (free pizza on Wednesdays, casual day on Fridays!). Valerie does not laugh out loud. Instead, she listens attentively while he explains why greasy takeout is, in fact, better than an extra ten grand a year.

## 8. KEEP A RECORD OF YOUR ACHIEVEMENTS.

Since Valerie was prepared, she has a list of reasons why she deserves that raise.

Valerie wraps it up by saying that she likes working there. The company is successful, her hard work has helped to contribute to that success, and it's important to her to work somewhere where she feels truly appreciated.

## Valerie's List

* I came up with a shortcut this year that saved the company two days in setup time. I figure that saved the company roughly $20,000 a project.
* When Steve, aka Steve the Stoner, got fired earlier this year for sniffing the paint thinner, I took up the slack. I know for a fact that my "being a trouper" saved the company a cool $50,000 in Steve's salary.
* I make about $8,000 less than the going rate. I deserve that, and more.

## 9. KNOW WHEN TO SAY YES.

Finally, Valerie tells Mr. Small the salary she wants. In a cool, calm, and collected voice, she says, "I want $90,000 a year." When Small gasps, Valerie doesn't flinch—she knows it's part of the game. He tells her he couldn't possibly—how about $77,000? Now she's got him negotiating. She counters with $85,000. He pretends to think it over, pretends to be anguished, pretends to look at his budget, and finally offers her $82,000. She accepts and they shake hands. Valerie makes a charming joke to offset any negotiating tension and walks away happy. Mission accomplished!

# Know your Car

check oil, water, motor & battery

your Bible on the road → Car Manual

store a jack, a spare tire & jumper cables in the trunk!

flashlight

funnel

Motor Oil

(grease monkey girls rule!)
be knowledgeable!

# MOBILIZATION

## mission:
### To keep your ride on the road and out of the shop.

Since the most highly trained Operative is prepared for any sticky situation, it's important to know what to do when your car has a meltdown. Let's face it, it's a major drag when your car dies, won't start, or you just don't have time (or the outfit) to change your flat. The easiest thing to do? Get a AAA membership.

But for those can-do chicas out there, learning how to change your oil, replace a tire, and jump-start your car gives you sweet liberation from overpriced mechanics. Think of it as a flip of the bird to all of those grease-covered jerks who've bilked you over the years.

Set yourself free, save 40 bucks, and learn how to:

## Change Your Oil
Car manufacturers recommend that you change your oil every 3,000 to 6,000 miles (or every three months).

## WHAT YOU NEED:

* Old clothes (we're not talking last season's dress) and rags
* The manual for your make of car (not all cars are alike)
* An oil filter wrench
* A crescent wrench
* Motor oil (ask a gas station attendant how many quarts your car requires)
* Oil filter
* Drip pan
* Small funnel

### Mobilization Tip #1

DO NOT dump your oil in the sewer, or anywhere else for that matter. The high levels of lead will contaminate drinking water and kill wildlife. (You don't want the deaths of harmless little critters on your conscience, do you?) Instead, take it to a service station or auto supply store where they will recycle it.

## HOW TO DO IT:

1. Park your car on a flat surface (set the emergency brake), and run it for a few minutes. Oil drains better when it's warm, but make sure you don't run it for too long—unless you're a masochist who's into hot oil burns.

2. Take the crescent wrench and shallow pan and crawl under the car. Find the oil plug under the engine block—it's on the underside of the oil pan.

3. Place the pan under the plug and unscrew it (counterclockwise) with the crescent wrench. Try to keep your arm raised so that oil doesn't run down it.

4. Watch the old oil rush out. *Note: The plug may fall into the pan along with the oil—don't worry.*

5. When all the oil has drained into the pan, screw the plug back in. Tighten it firmly, but don't strip the threads.

6. From above or below your car (depending on the make), find the oil filter and wrap the oil filter wrench around it. Unscrew the oil filter carefully, since it's full of (what else?) oil, and empty it in the drip pan.

7. Dip your fingertip into the new quart of oil, and lube the circular edge of the new filter (where it touches the metal engine surface).

8. Screw the new filter in with your hand, and tighten it firmly without overtightening.

9. Open your oil cap, which is situated on top of your engine (usually in plain view), drop the funnel in, and pour in the new oil. Replace the oil cap, and wipe up any oil drips on the engine.

10. Revel in your newly discovered inner Grease Monkey.

# Change Your Tire

## WHAT YOU NEED:

* A jack
* A properly inflated spare tire
* Lug wrench (with sockets that fit your wheel)
* Flashlight (because you know this will happen at night, for maximum inconvenience)
* Gloves and a tarp or small blanket (to keep your hands and knees from getting dirty)

### HOW TO DO IT:

1. Make sure you're in a safe place (i.e., out of the way of traffic, not on a hill or incline). Put your hazard lights and emergency brake on.

2. Loosen the lug nuts on the tire you're changing. Sometimes they're hidden under the hubcap, sometimes not. Use your lug wrench or jack handle to pry the hubcap off if necessary, then turn each nut counterclockwise with your wrench. *Note: Leave the lug nut on the threaded shaft.*

3. Position the jack on a solid foundation, and raise it so that it just touches the car. Once you've got it in place, continue raising the car until there's enough room for you to slide the flat tire off.

4. Remove the lug nuts by hand, and pull the flat tire off.

5. Slide the spare into place, and tighten the lug nuts in opposite pairs so the wheel is firmly mounted.

6. Release the jack so the car is back on the ground, then tighten the lug nuts securely. Remove the jack.

7. Drive to a garage. The spare is not designed to last long (or to go at high speeds, so keep it nice and easy).

## Jump-start Your Car
### WHAT YOU NEED:

* A set of jumper cables—100% copper, heavy (4 to 8) gauge, and at least 10 feet long
* Old toothbrush or wire brush
* A car that's running

### HOW TO DO IT:

1. Make sure both cars are turned off and parked side by side or facing hood to hood.

2. If there is white, green, or yellow corrosion around the terminals, clean it off with the wire brush.

3. Attach the positive cable end (red handle) to the positive terminal on the dead battery; then attach the other positive cable end to the battery in the car you're getting the jump from.

4. Attach the negative cable end (black handle) to the negative terminal on the battery in the running car, then attach the other negative cable end to the engine block or frame (an unpainted metal surface away from the battery) of the car with the dead battery.

5. Start the car that's providing the jump start.

6. Start your car. If your car doesn't immediately start, let the other car run for about five minutes, then try to start your car again.

7. Once your car is running, remove the cables starting in reverse (first the cable clamp attached to your car frame, then the negative cable clamp attached to the battery in the starting car, then the positive cable clamp on that battery, and finally, the positive clamp on your battery).

8. Thank the person who helped you, then drive your car for a while to make sure the battery is fully charged.

# MORNING AFTER

Too many martinis—shaken, not stirred—can make for a scary morning after. Mr. HotPants from the karaoke bar doesn't look so sparkly in the harsh A.M., does he? On top of this minor complication, you're also struggling with a hangover that could stop a hollow-tipped bullet. It happens to the best of us. Unfortunately, life's missions wait for no one, so you'd better find a fix, and fast.

There's no feel-better-quick cure for the pounding head, nausea, dry mouth, and other nonstop fun that come with a hangover. But there are a few things you can do to minimize the effects of a first-class bender.

1. Before you pass out—uh . . . *fall asleep*—down as much water or Gatorade as you can guzzle. It'll keep you from getting dehydrated. Also, pop a multivitamin that has minerals—it'll help your poor, mistreated body process all that alcohol.

2. Don't mix your alcohol.

## A Little Story About Mixing Your Liquor

Lola goes out to meet some friends after work at Le Bar, where she downs a couple of **tequila** (to-kill-ya) gimlets. They decide to have dinner, and our gal has a couple of glasses of **red wine** with her meal. (A little wine doesn't count, does it?) After eating, the troops decide that the night is still young, so they move the party to another bar, where an already drunk Lola has a couple of **beers**. See Lola having fun. See Lola crawl up the stairs to her apartment. See Lola praying to the porcelain god, Ralph. See Lola wake up feeling like someone smacked her over the head with a two-by-four. Point made? We thought so.

### Morning After Tip #1

Sugary drinks (anything made with liqueurs) will hit you harder the morning after. Too much sugar in the stomach mixes with the alcohol and makes for one sick party girl.

3. Post-hangover food theories abound. Eating bananas the morning after helps some recover. Others say eating tomato sauce (say, with spaghetti or lasagna) does the trick. Still others claim that a big greasy meal, like Mexican food or fast food, is the way to go. One thing's for sure: Eating before you go to sleep helps the most.

4. Caffeine comes in many forms—tea, coffee, soda, to name a few—and may make you feel better.

5. One more time: Eating while drinking is a smart (and yummy) way to lessen the effects of alcohol.

6. Take a bath to sweat out the toxins.

7. Do like the French, and down a glass of water after every alcoholic drink.

8. The best way to prevent a hangover? Don't drink too much, you putz.

## Around-the-World Cures

It's been said that Russian women who've downed too much vodka the night before drink fizzy cabbage juice for hangovers. In Germany, some say marinated fish is great for the morning after. The Chinese sip kudzu tea to help them sober up. Mexican partiers swear by menudo, a soup made from tripe and hominy.

### Morning After Tip #2

Some studies say that taking aspirin, acetaminophen, or ibuprofen while you've been drinking can be hazardous to your health. Painkillers are metabolized through the liver, and we all know what alcohol does to a person's liver, don't we? Use your own judgment.

Some say **"hair of the dog"** (drinking more alcohol) is the best way to get over a hangover. Actually, it's a good way to guarantee that you'll become an alcoholic.

# PEE STANDING UP

**mission:**
**To answer nature's call while on the go.**

It's a cruel world, and it's even crueler when you've just downed a gallon of $H_2O$ and there's not a ladies' room in sight. Sadly, some businesses deny customers the right to use their bathrooms. Frankly, we think such stinginess should be outlawed, and all restroom keys should be liberated for the people. But hey, we're not in charge of the Ladies' Room Laws, and unfortunately, neither are you. That means it's your job to convince the Keepers of the Key that you are a risk they should be willing to take. Here's a list of our favorite tactics:

## 1. THE MEDICAL ALERT

Buy one of those medical bracelets they sell at drugstores. Keep it in your car for emergencies like these. Calmly tell the employee that you have a serious medical condition that could be aggravated if you don't use the bathroom immediately, and show them your wrist (which is now clad in said bracelet). If they still don't budge, ask for their card and threaten them with a lawsuit. It probably won't work but it'll at least be satisfying.

## 2. THE PREGNANCY PLOY
Play the sympathy card and tell them you're pregnant.

## For the Truly Desperate

The worse the neighborhood, the longer you'll have to hold it since businesses in these areas are less likely to let you use their rest rooms. So hang on until you get to a safer area.

It's kind of scary in a survivalist sort of way, but you could always carry around an empty glass jar in your car for this particular emergency. *Note: For the sake of your next passenger, you must empty and wash it when you're done. Otherwise, you could seriously scar a friendship.*

# What Every Girl Should Know—How to Pee Standing Up
Let's face it, who wants to squat over a gas station toilet anyway, praying your legs don't give out and smack you down on a skanky toilet? Buy a Freshette or TravelMate, and keep it in your car's Bug-Out Bag (see Hit the Road). These nifty gadgets enable you to go standing up, without even pulling your pants down. Alternatively, learn to pee standing up—who knew? *Note: Practice makes perfect, so hit the shower for some pretend emergencies.*

## Here's the drill:
1. Clean your hands with soap and water or a towelette.
2. Pull your pants down a few inches or hike your skirt up and move

your panties away from the crotch. Pee stains on your outfit are no fun.

3. Make a V with your pointer finger and your middle finger, and, well, spread yourself. Spread the inner lips of your vagina (labia minora, FYI) with your V.

4. Lift (this is key) and pee. *Note: You run the risk of dribbling if you don't follow this step perfectly.*

5. Wipe yourself off. Adjust your clothing, wash your hands, and strut out like the bad Mama Jama you are.

Most chain restaurants and hotel lobbies have rest rooms that the public can use.

# PINK SLIP

### mission:
**Getting the ax—and bringing it down—with no blood and a minimum of tears.
Bonus points for successful office-supply raid on way out of building.**

## Getting the Ax

If you're a girl with a wide streak of the nonconformist (our favorite streak), chances are you'll find yourself on the business end of a pink slip one day. It's not that you're a failure; it's just that you couldn't bring yourself to say "Super Size" with the perkiness your drive-thru manager expected. Time to move on, and no need to torture yourself over it. In fact, you're in fine company (with heads of state, rock stars, and, yes, even the author of this book). Instead of feeling like a loser, try to see the sunny side: This could be the change you've been needing.

Give yourself a few days to indulge in the Just-Been-Fired Blues (complaining to friends over a margarita or two never hurts), but then move on to finding a new paycheck. (See "J.O.B Blues.") If your former job involved a skanky boss (see "Boss from Hell"), begin your tell-all memoir to exact revenge.

## GOOD THINGS ABOUT GETTING FIRED

* Now you can move on to your dream job.
* Now you can reassess your life—hey, no nine-to-five to keep you from moving to another state.
* Best of all, now you can collect unemployment. (Although you won't be living high on the hog, trust me.)

# The Turnaround: Giving the Ax

Handing out a pink slip is never easy. Even the most hard-boiled operative has a heart and hates to see a grown-up cry. But a job is a job and if someone's not up to snuff, you have to give him or her the heave-ho. Think of it this way: If someone's consistently not pulling his weight, chances are everyone else is working overtime to pull it for him. It's your obligation to fix the problem.

Of course, there's a wrong way and a right way to go about ditching someone. Here's a primer.

## THE SETUP

When he started, Dick seemed like the perfect receptionist: well-mannered, energetic, and eager to please. But lately, Dick has become the employee from hell. He leaves the office for hours without telling anyone, makes spectacular mistakes when copying reports, and usually gives you completely illegible phone messages. You've warned Dick that his job performance, well, sucks and have

### The Hiring 1-2-3s: Stop, Look, and Listen

The next time you have a position to fill, don't talk too much during the job interview. Instead, explain the job's requirements and spend the rest of the time letting your potential employee talk about his or her last job and boss, her skills and experience, etc. Really listen to what's being said. That way you'll get a better handle on who it is you're hiring. You may even learn how to stop hiring loser employees like Dick.

given him time to clean up his act. (The last phone message he gave you had six digits.) You've documented your complaints and are being reasonable with your expectations. ("Seven digits at least, Dick. Please.") But Dick's performance hasn't changed, and he's clearly not taking the job or your warning seriously. Check your employee handbook and federal laws to make sure you're within your rights to give Dick the old boot.

## Do's and Don'ts for Letting Someone Go

**Do:**

* Speak honestly and very clearly about the reasons for the discharge. ("Did you really have to high-five the CEO?")
* Ask someone else to sit in (preferably a member of Human Resources) as support for Dick.
* Explain any severance packages, benefits that continue, or job placement counseling in clear and concise terms.
* Have at hand a list of company property (keys, Xerox card, etc.) that Dick has to return. No one wants him coming back for last-minute supplies.

**Don't:**

* Get personal by saying things that could humiliate the guy. (For example, "Are you a total moron or just a slacker?")
* Give him any hope of a turnaround. It's counterproductive , and you've made your final decision. Tell him firmly that the purpose of the meeting is to let him go.
* Insist that he leave the building as soon as your talk is done. Instead, give him time to pack his personal effects and leave during a low-visibility period (after-hours or on a weekend).
* Sabotage the employee's chances of getting a job elsewhere. Discuss with him a "story" you will stick to when called as a reference.

# SCAM CITY

## mission:

**To scam a good deal while staying on the right side of the law.**

There are discounts available everywhere for the asking—but the point is, you have to ask. Perhaps you've never heard of the following hustles, or perhaps you know them like the back of your manicured hand. Here goes:

## Hustles We Love

1. **The Kid's Fare.** Order movie tickets by phone and get the child's fare (usually half price). When you go to pick them up, the ticket taker rarely looks to see what type of ticket you have, so you get the movie at half price. If you get busted, act dumb. You may have to pay the higher fare—or the guy may actually be charmed by your act.

**2. The Taste Tester.** Score your Saturday tea at a superstore or market that specializes in "free taste setups." You can make a meal out of their samples and do your shopping. *Note: We like the mini quiches.*

**3. The Press Pass.** Scoring this is like having the Super Gold Pass to the entertainment world. It's also the ultimate in scammer accessories. If you have to work for it, *c'est la vie. Note: An alternative to a press pass is to start a band, magazine, or become a club promoter or DJ. These are more valid ways to get the key to the city.*

Taste Tester

**4. The Happy Return.** The golden rule of drag queens and stylists alike: Buy clothes, wear them once, and return them. Your wardrobe will be drop-dead fabulous, and your bank account will breathe a sigh of relief. Make sure you don't remove the tags. (Tuck them in where they're not visible.) Do not get pit stains (or any other kind of stain) on the clothes, and make sure they don't stink after you wear them. *Note: This hustle is not recommended if you tend to get too attached to your clothes to return them.*

**5. The Seat Saver.** If there's a long line at the movie theater, have your friends wait in line, then go up to the ticket seller and buy tickets for everyone. Go back to your friends, and give them their tickets. While they wait, go up to the front of the line, and find some unsuspecting guy. Give him your most stunning smile, and ask if you can join him.

Once you're in the theater, save seats for you and your friends (it helps if you have coats or a newspaper). This way, everyone can sit together. *Note: This also works if you're solo and just don't feel like waiting in line.*

## Scam City Tip #1

**Ask and Ye Shall Receive.** Ask for discounts everywhere. One shrewd subject we know tried this as an experiment. For an entire week, every time she paid for something, she asked if she could get it, well, cheaper. She explained that she was a good customer who had been frequenting the place for a while. Amazingly enough, it worked. She scored discounts and deals in places she never expected—from the phone company (free minutes for 6 months) to the dry cleaners. Try this and see if it works for you. *Note: The main reason this strategy works is that companies don't want you to leave them for their competitor. So if you're dealing with a corporation—say, a phone company that offers long distance—explain that you think your bill is too high and that the competitor is offering better rates. Then wait to see if they start dealing. Play hardball and don't take no for an answer.*

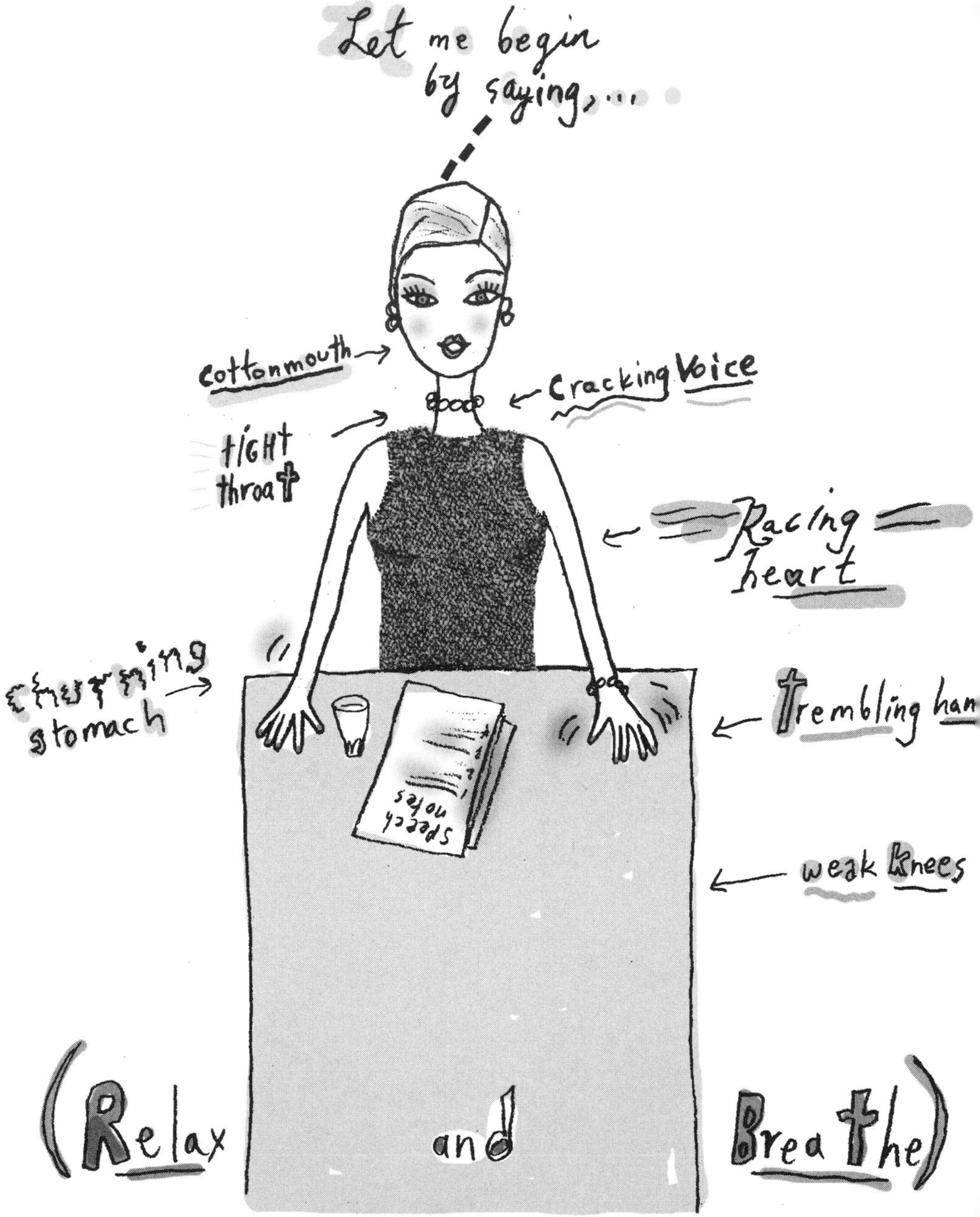

Let me begin by saying, . . .
cottonmouth
Cracking Voice
tight throat
Racing heart
churning stomach
Trembling han
speech notes
weak knees
(Relax and Breathe)

# SCHMOOZING, SOCIALIZING, AND SURVIVING THE SPOTLIGHT

**mission:**

To work a room, a Rolodex, or your dad's bowling club
until someone gives you your damn dream job.

Every job huntress should know how to schmooze, even if she works the counter at McDonald's—wait, make that *especially* if she works the counter at McDonald's.

If you are a successful schmoozer, you will expand not only your circle of acquaintances but also the number of groovy opportunities that life presents you. If you are a bad schmoozer, you will come across as a big fake, which only makes people feel creepy.

There are no Top Secret Tricks to being an effective networker—just six simple rules.

1. **Have a firm handshake.** Nothing gives a worse first impression than a wet-noodle grasp.

2. **Be subtle.** When introducing yourself to Big Bill, don't blurt out that you've been trying to land a job at his company. Take your time, and be sincere.

3. **Overcome your shyness.** Everyone is nervous about meeting new people— learn to power through your jitters. It helps to be direct: "Hi, my name is Ruby, and I wanted to introduce myself." Realize that even the most successful person can be a little timid when it comes to meeting new people.

4. **Find common ground.** Take a cue from your surroundings. In a bookstore, talk books and writers; in a gallery, talk art or people-watching; at a football game, talk sports or athletes; at a dinner, talk restaurants or food.

5. **Be tactful.** If you're talking to the head of BigAss Records, don't ask her out for a cup of coffee or tell her your little sister is in a band. (Believe me, she doesn't have the time and hears the band pitch from roughly half the people she meets.)

6. **Keep it real.** Nothing is worse than talking to a scary phony. Remember, you're trying to build contacts for life, so let the real you come through.

## Great Ways to Network

* Cold-call (you'd be surprised how well this works)
* Volunteer (at clubs, committees, neighborhood meetings, conferences, environmental groups, shelters)
* Intern (at a magazine, film, or record company, or any other business you're interested in)
* E-mail (many companies list their employees' e-mail addresses online)

## Survive the Spotlight

If you're a successful schmoozer, more than likely you'll climb ever higher on the career ladder. And when you reach an appropriately dizzying height, it will happen: you'll be asked to speak in public. Yes, there will come a time when you'll be forced to address an audience—and you will survive.

## THE SYMPTOMS

Churning stomach, nausea, sweating, using the bathroom a lot, hyperventilating, racing heart, weak knees, cottonmouth, cracking voice, vomiting, trembling hands, tight throat. Sound fun so far?

## THE CURE

* Take deep, slow, relaxing breaths from your stomach.

* Realize the experience isn't as terrifying as you think. Instead of imagining the worst thing that could happen, think of the best. (And so what if the worst thing does happen? It only makes for a better story to tell your friends.)

* Relax your throat by yawning.

* Make eye contact with the foreheads or hairlines of your audience (sometimes eyes can be too distracting). *Note: For some speakers, it helps to make eye contact. Once you're more experienced, you'll find that it helps to engage your audience and forget about yourself.*

* Perform more often. The more you do it, the better you feel.

* Don't mistake adrenaline for fear.

{ Jane Bond pad

← bamboo

↑ thrift store glass w/ apple martini

← foreign maps
Paris

{ Mata hari pad

← peacock feather

lacquer furniture

Decor su casa

{ Cleopatra pad

← Columns w/cherubs

mirrors mucho

Rose Oil

← for the tub

{ emma peel pad

faux zebra rug

bowler hat →

# STYLE PILE MAKEOVER

**To breathe some worldly life into your deadbeat digs.**

You think of your home as your shelter—a refuge where you can escape from weird bosses and annoying friends into your own singular space. Still, you also want it to be a place where you can entertain comfortably, whether it's several people or that one special guest.

Here are a few themes inspired by our favorite stylin' heroines that we think make for supreme swankiness.

## Survivalista Styles That Inspire

We've collected a few tricks to ensure that your shelter is *trés* chic. Just remember: A shelter should delight, not bite.

### JANE BOND'S BACHELOR PAD

Never heard of James's half sister? That's because she kept a lower profile than her flashy brother—proving she was the better Double Agent after all.

139

## THREE DECOR TIPS

\* Pick two primary colors, such as yellow and red, and use them as inspiration for your space. Paint the walls yellow and make red slipcovers for your furniture, accenting the room with eggplant-colored throw pillows, glasses, vases, or picture frames.

\* Find an old vanity, display case, or vintage bar, and make it the centerpiece of the living room. Customize it with paint, fringe, framed photos, and a vase filled with flowers. Keep it stocked with your favorite liquor, teas, Japanese crackers, cashews, spicy olives, and a collection of funky thrift-store drinking glasses.

\* To give your shelter that worldly *je ne sais quoi*, hang bamboo curtains in the windows and old city maps of Paris, London, and Berlin on the walls.

ESSENTIAL GADGET: camera-watch for recording all visitors to your shelter. Extra Survivalista points if visitors are unaware of documentation.

SCENT TIP: When contemplating your next operation, use Stay Focused\* in a water diffuser to enhance your thoughts.

DRINK OF CHOICE: apple martini

SUGGESTED COLORS: black, dark red, green, eggplant, and yellow

**\*Stay Focused:** Combine 5 drops of pure, essential clary sage oil, 5 drops basil oil, 5 drops lavender oil, and 2 drops geranium oil with water in the diffuser's bowl.

## MATA HARI'S MYSTERIOUS LAIR

Mata Hari was an ineffective Double Agent in most respects, except when it came to style.

### THREE DECOR TIPS

\* Buy inexpensive small blue-and-white Chinese vases (from Pier 1, Cost Plus, Chinatown) and fill them with peacock feathers (available at any crafts store), sticks, fresh herbs, dried flowers, or inexpensive red carnations. Place them in groupings around your shelter, along with ferns (or other houseplants with pretty leaves) placed in larger Chinese and terra-cotta pots.

* Buy sari fabric or chinoiserie (shiny Chinese fabric embroidered with flowers, birds, etc.), and use it for curtains, pillows (you should have lots of huge pillows on your bed or sofa for that ultraseductive, exotic mood), or bedspreads. Also, get a white shag rug for your floor and faux leopard or tiger fur to drape over the bed, sofa, or chairs.

* Lacquer your dressers, tables, and chairs in red and black, and change any hardware to Asian-themed knobs and pulls.

**\*In the Mood:**
Combine 10 drops each of jasmine, rose, and ylang ylang oil in a 2-ounce dark glass bottle with spray top. Add 2 ounces of water and shake well before spraying.

ESSENTIAL GADGET: voice-disguising telephone for that weekly call to your favorite deliverin' drugstore for condoms, cake, and cosmetics

SCENT TIP: Spray In the Mood\* in the air when you're feeling frisky—alone or with company.

DRINK OF CHOICE: sex on the beach

SUGGESTED COLORS: turquoise, crimson red, gold, ebony, and pale orange

## CLEOPATRA'S CASA D'AMOUR

Cleopatra didn't just decorate a room—she conquered it (just like she did a certain Roman emperor).

### THREE DECOR TIPS

* Hang sheer fabric or mosquito netting above your bed (decked with white Egyptian cotton sheets and white satin pillows) to create a veiled effect. A saucy picture—preferably on black velvet—of an amorous couple looks particularly fine hanging above the bed. Keep the lighting seductive with bedside lamps and candles.

* Turn your bathroom into an alluring grotto with potted palms on columns, plaster statues of cherubs or naked women, dim lighting, gold towels, and a satiny shower curtain. If you can, epoxy glass beads in purple, black, and gold

**141**

along the rim of your tub to create a spilling-over effect.

* Mirrors, mirrors, mirrors—in the kitchen, living room, and especially the bedroom.

ESSENTIAL GADGET: the Clapper, for instant mood lighting. (Your date won't have a chance.)

SCENT TIP: Cleopatra's famous seduction of Mark Antony began when she scented the sails of her ship with rose oil. Try Queen Bee* in the tub to feel like you rule.

DRINK OF CHOICE: cream and Amaretto

SUGGESTED COLORS: purple, black, gold, milky white, and rose

**\*Queen Bee:**
Put 5 drops each of pure, essential oils (such as sandalwood, ylang ylang, and patchouli) in a full tub of water, and mix well with your hand before getting in.

## PATTY HEARST'S PREPPY HIDEAWAY

First she was a deb, then a revolutionary. This is Survivalista home decor—Symbionese Liberation Army-style.

### THREE DECOR TIPS

* Paint your walls lilac, the trim (molding, windows, baseboard) in shell pink, and hang photos of female style icons (like old-school actress Ava Gardner, diva Mary J. Blige, or writer Colette) in cheap frames you've painted chocolate brown.

* Hang window curtains in pink camouflage trimmed with green ribbon.

* Alternate your use of colors (pink kitchen cupboards, green knobs, brown bedspread, pink pillows, green lamp shades) throughout your shelter.

ESSENTIAL GADGET: caller ID to determine identity of potential admirers, stalkers, and/or credit card company employees (See Beat the Bank)

SCENT TIP: Feeling overly suspicious? Massage Born Yesterday* into your temples and body.

DRINK OF CHOICE: surfer on acid (Malibu rum, Jaegermeister, pineapple juice,

grenadine—chilled and served as a shot)

SUGGESTED COLORS: army green, shell pink, camel, lilac, and chocolate brown

*Born Yesterday:
Blend 4 ounces almond oil with 15 drops each of lavender and jasmine oil.

## EMMA PEEL'S MOD LODGE

Independent and chic, she Avenged bad style everywhere.

### THREE DECOR TIPS

* Paint your living room white with black trim, and hang black-and-white polka-dotted curtains in your living room windows.

* Keep the room looking minimal with white slip-covered furniture (with pink-and-black polka-dotted pillows), a faux zebra-skin rug, and thrift-store tables that you've stripped and stained white.

* Hang framed posters of '60s British films on the walls. Add a hat rack, and hang one bowler and one umbrella on it.

ESSENTIAL GADGET: the Fogmaster for instant Jolly-Old atmosphere

SCENT TIP: After a busy day of subversive activity, clear your mind at night with Thoughts Be-Gone.*

DRINK OF CHOICE: lemon drop, because you gotta love the Peel

SUGGESTED COLORS: black, white, pink, gray, and green

*Thoughts Be-Gone:
In 1/2 cup of warm water add 6 to 8 drops of eucalyptus oil. Place by your bed when you're ready to sleep.

(been done wrong)
speak no evil
Good Friends are the Sweetest Revenge
I hate you! You broke my heart Karl. I hope you miss me!!!
write & burn a slam letter (do NOT mail it!)

# SWEET REVENGE

**mission:**

**To feel the joy of payback without becoming creepier than your target.**

Ever been dumped? Had someone spread lies about you? (Even worse, had them spread the true stuff?) Maybe you didn't get that promotion because your coworker took credit for your hard work? If you answered yes to any of the above questions, then you have probably been pissed off enough to crave the bittersweet taste of revenge.

We'd love to give you a no-nonsense list of ways to extract revenge— a really great car-keying, phone-tampering, new-girlfriend-stalking list— but we won't. Thing is, hurting other people is dumb. Worse, it's not that satisfying. So even though you think your boyfriend's car windows deserve to be smashed, heaving that brick will only brand you a psycho and him as the victim. Of course, the desire to disfigure his car is totally natural (and, in fact, can make for excellent fantasy), but what you decide to do with that emotion is what makes you different from an animal. Meaning, that's what our brains are for: to stop and consider the consequences before we attack.

When you stoop to someone else's low standards, you're letting people know you're hurt—and desperate to be noticed: Jerk: 10, You: 0.

The lowdown: Revenge looks great on TV. In real life, it doesn't look or feel so good.

So what'll make you feel better?

How 'bout:

* Moving into a fabulous new apartment.
* Hanging with friends who believe what you say (and not what they hear).
* Becoming spectacularly successful at your job.
* Landing an Italian lover; and knowing that while you can move on and become a better person, that loser who hurt you will always be stuck in the muck of his own rottenness.

### Sweet Revenge Tip #1
Instead of sending that hate letter to the person who hurt your feelings, send it to your girlfriends so they can add their own slams. Or write it just for yourself and make a ritual out of burning it. Just the act should make you feel better.

Of course, none of this means you should just roll over. Letting people know you're hurt is really important, not to mention an excellent excuse for a martini-soaked blues-fest with your friends. But has anyone's mind ever been changed by an extreme act of revenge? Sorry, but no. Revenge is about you. And you, my friend, should move on.

The best form of revenge? Feeling and looking good. Just make sure the creep who hurt you hears (from you or your friends) about how fabulous you've become. It'll drive the jerk crazy. Now *that's* payback.

## A Simple Spell

Before you head out to your local magick shop for a nasty little spell to cast, think twice. Wiccans* believe in something called the Threefold Law, which means that everything you do comes back to you three times worse. Like karma, it's about the energy you put out.

*another name for witches or anyone else who follows the nature-based, pagan religion

A-List Tactics
be a regular
call ahead
use a fake name
go on a slow night - mon., tues.
hello, I mad
a reservation
My name is Blaine Hilton.

# TABLE FOR TWO

**mission:**

**To hustle your way into the hottest feed spot in town
without having to wait tables there.**

Sure, we know that those of us with real style don't need to follow the herd to the latest quasi-fusion-bistro just to prove that we're in the know. Then again, sometimes you want to see what all the fuss is about. Sometimes you want to see if Tom Cruise really does eat there. And sometimes you just want to taste the damn pineapple-glazed cinnamon-infused pork chop for yourself.

Whatever the reason, you can bet that getting past that nasty little prig with the power complex and the reservations list will be a challenge. Luckily, we love a good challenge, especially those that involve a possible encounter with Tom Cruise and/or food (not necessarily in that order). Here's a list of some of our best haute cuisine strategies.

## Tactical Maneuvers

1. Become a regular. You don't have to be Madonna to get the table you want. Maître d's and servers will go out of their way to make their best customers (read: most regular customers) comfortable.

2. Don't be a shrew. Rudeness (as in "I can get you fired!" or the hands-down favorite of maître d's everywhere: "Do you know who I am?!") will get you nowhere fast, whether you're complaining about not being able to get a reservation or griping about the wait. Call ahead and tell the reservations person you'd appreciate being put on the cancellation list. Call back to ask if anything has opened up. And be flexible—especially while you're building a relationship. If they offer you a six o'clock table, jump on it. You can always linger for a while as the glitterati come in.

3. Go on a slow night. Obviously, some restaurants are packed every night of the week, while others count Thursday through Sunday as their busy nights. Find out when their slowest night is and call ahead to get reservations for that evening.

## Spread the Wealth

When all else fails and you absolutely have to get into Chez Fancy Fork, try a little old-fashioned palm greasing. Go to the restaurant even though you don't have a reservation. Be very discreet, and slip the maître d' a twenty (or a fifty, depending on how popular the restaurant is) while asking if there are any tables available for that night. You'll probably find yourself seated within minutes.

4. Give a fake last name. Hey, we're not above a white lie now and then when faced with a particularly stubborn situation. Just don't be too heavy-handed about it; stay away from the obvious surnames

like Rockefeller and Trump. A less well-known family name (whose members you just happen to slightly resemble) can be amazingly effective. Experiment and see which name works for you.

5. Get to know the maître d'. If you've gotten cozy with the person who seats people, you will find yourself getting a table faster than people who have been waiting longer than you. Fact: This works at the diner down the street, too.

When you do score that reservation, make sure you request the table you want, or at least rule out the one you don't want. Otherwise, you may find yourself seated in that lovely spot across from the toilets. Bummer.

## The Flip Side of Reservations

If you're going to be late for—or entirely miss—your reservation, always call to let the restaurant know. A reservation is an unwritten contract. If they think they're getting a party of eight, they will buy extra food, and possibly even ask an extra server to come in. If you expect to be treated well, return the favor.

And if you arrive for your reservation on time and the table isn't ready, it's perfectly acceptable for the maître d' to ask you to wait in the bar. Waiting fifteen minutes is fine; longer than that and the restaurant should buy you a drink. After all, they're making extra money by overbooking their tables and having people buy $8 cocktails in their bar while they wait. Many restaurants do this automatically, but usually you have to say something and call it to their attention—nicely.

Tweedy + Leather Trimmed

sensible for **Job Interview**

sporty cheeky tote

playful for **1rst Date** (daytime)

# UNDERCOVER

## mission:
### Choosing the right cover, color, and cleavage for any setting.

Think about it—where would Gwen Stefani be without her ever-changing fashion statements? India Arie without her 'do-wraps? Sure, they'd probably all be on top anyway, but it's their style that sets them apart. Clothes may not make the diva, but they can be a great shorthand for communicating their fabulousness. Fact: Sometimes you can judge a book by its miniskirt.

Thing is, you want to be sure you know the right shorthand for the right setting. Let's review a few classic situations, along with recommended style tips:

## Situation: Meet the Parents

1. Leave the "hoochie" at home, and keep those boobs under wraps. You don't need to flaunt your sexual power over their offspring by wearing your skintight best.

2. No siren-red lipstick. You're better off with I'm-ready-to-bear-your-grandchildren pink.

3. The more conservative, the better. Don't go overboard with a Mormon routine, but be respectful and wear clothes that say, "I'm-prepared to suck up as much as necessary."

## Situation: Job Interview

1. Tailor your dress to fit the workplace. What flies at your record label job (T-shirts, leather, vintage clothing) will bomb at an investment house. So keep your piercings to yourself.

2. Shine your shoes and keep jewelry to a minimum: a watch (to show you're timely), an understated necklace if you like, and a simple pair of small hoop or stud earrings. (Dangly earrings, for some reason, just scream "unreliable" in a job interview.)

3. A simple job interview uniform: A boat-neck shirt with 3/4 sleeves or a long-sleeved button-down shirt goes great with a pair of dress pants or a knee-length skirt. Top it all off with a little blazer. Tip: Fitted velvet blazers are great for instant style and won't frighten prospective employers. Find them at Loehmann's or other discount designer stores; if you're on the small side, shop the little boy's section at Goodwill. (The sleeves might be a little short, but that'll show off your watch.)

## Situation: First Date

1. Don't put all the goods on display the first night. Instead, try to balance your masculine and feminine energies—that way you're prepared for whichever direction the date might turn (i.e., midnight make-out or escape at eight. See Ditch the Date).

2. Try this: red lipstick but no eye shadow; low-slung pants with high heels; a chamois-colored A-line leather skirt with a white T-shirt.

3. Do your nails, but don't go for the fancy manicure. That way if you don't like the guy, you won't feel like you worked too hard for nothing.

## Situation: Wedding Day (Someone Else's!)

1. Check the invite for the time and location of the ceremony and reception. A garden party is more informal than a church ceremony. You can wear colors, prints, even black. Dresses are pre-ferred, but a skirt and pretty top are fine, too. Leave the stilettos at home. Tip: Heels are hell at those lawn parties.

2. Don't compete with the wedding party or try to upstage the bride (no white!). If you're unsure of the dress code, feel free to dress up, but leave the plunging tops and microminis at home.

3. Now is your chance to wear a really big hat, which is, let's face it, an oppor-tunity that doesn't present itself often enough in life.

## Situation: Impress the Clients

1. A little style savvy is OK, but now is not the time to get trendy. Instead, your look should say, "You can trust me with your money, Honey."

2. Double-check the important details, like that your shirt is ironed, the creases in your pants are straight, your shirt collar is flat, there aren't any loose threads or but-tons hanging, and your face is clear of any wandering mascara or runaway lipstick.

3. Make sure your shoes are in great shape. Scuffed or uneven heels, tired-look-ing leather, and cheap shoe materials are not signs of success.

# VELVET ROPE

**To boldly cross the line that turns you from a "one of them" into a "one of us."**

Industry parties, new nightclubs, society weddings, and invite-only restaurant openings all present a sticky problem: How does a conniving chica get on the other side of the velvet rope? Barring sleeping with the person who does the door (one word: *skanky*), here's a little how-to that will whisk you from the D-list (Don't Come Back) to the A-list (Always Nice to See Ya).

## Tactical Maneuvers
### 1. LOOK LIKE YOU BELONG
Nervous body language and stammering will get you nowhere fast. Self-confidence and self-possession will open doors. If you look like you need to get in, you probably won't.

### 2. ARRIVE IN STYLE
Don't pull up in your 1981 Toyota Tercel hatchback. Instead, take a cab (*trés chic*) or

## DOOR GUY STRATEGY #1: THE WHAMMY

We know a New York club-hopper who uses this technique with a 75% success rate. As she approaches a club with a long line out front, she looks directly at the door guy (that's the Whammy). She maintains her look in an important and meaningful way ("We both know you should know who I am, so don't make me get you fired") as she walks purposefully toward the front of the line. To pull this off, imagine that you are Angelina Jolie (or whoever you pretend to be when you give your bathroom-mirror acceptance speech) while you stare him down. If he dares to stop you, the jig is probably up. To save face, tell him that your party is already inside and you just wanted to join them.

go with a friend who has an SUV (trés bad for the environment but looks money nonetheless). *Note: Showing up on foot looks like you couldn't afford a ride.*

## 3. GET TO KNOW THE POWERS THAT BE

We aren't suggesting that you should sleep your way into any party—a trashy and (frankly) amateurish ploy. No, a better alternative is to get to know the promoter. To get on the list, call the club that day or the night before, and ask to speak with the manager or promoter. Once you've got him on the phone, convince him of your fabulousness. If that doesn't work, next time call him and lie and convince him you're someone else. (See Door Guy Strategy #3; see also Tactical Maneuver #7 from Table for Two).

### Velvet Rope Tip #1

The old guest list switcheroo is one of our favorite tricks. While you're out of sight, have your partner in crime hang out where the guest lists are kept until she sees a name on the list. When she does, she'll come tell you what it is. You approach the keepers of the list, give that name (guest lists always have a +1), and the two of you are in like Flynn. *Note: This trick always works better at small clubs; at larger venues, list keepers are more likely to ask for an ID.*

## 4. PROMOTE YOURSELF

Act like you work there. This may enable you to glide through the front door, but more likely than not, you'll have to stop, drop, and roll through a back entrance. Observe the staff's comings and goings and enter where they do. Be sure to watch out for security.

## 5. TRAVEL IN PACKS

A girl posse is much more appealing to a door guy than a gal flying solo or one who surrounds herself with a pack of guys. Promoters want females in their clubs, reasoning accurately that male clubgoers will then spend more money.

## 6. FIND A FRIEND

While waiting on the other side of the velvet rope, glance at your watch. Give a friendly acknowledgment to the gorillas manning the door, and let them know you're just waiting on a friend. Give yourself about 5 or 10 minutes, then look inside the party, and yell to someone inside, "There you are! I've been waiting out here." Then, adopting your best impatient diva attitude, glide inside.

**159**

## 7. A STAR IS BORN

Tell the promoter you're the assistant to (insert minor celebrity name here), who would like to visit the club that evening. *Note: Do not decide to go for broke and name a major star: a) They probably already know Gwyneth's assistant, and you'll only look stupid; and b) you'll have to show up that night with Gwyneth, who's 99.9% certain not to take your calls. We suggest the daughter of a political VIP, which no self-respecting nightlifer would ever recognize. Enlist a friend who has major confidence to play the part of the senator's daughter, and toast each other once inside the club—here's to being sneaky!*

## SO THERE YOU HAVE IT.

You've learned how to throw a party, deal with an evil landlord and fix even the most heinous of friendship snafus. Your fridge is stocked with gourmet snacks and your wallet's full of money (okay, maybe not full, but at least it's not totally empty). And you can pee standing up better than a lumberjack at a dive bar. (Or maybe you're just reading this page because you're the sort of girl who likes to check out the end of a book before she reads the beginning, in which case, see what you've missed out on? Go back! Read!) Now go out and kick some ass, like the cool girl you know you are.